Cheerful Madness

How eleven couples made it to marriage!

Jo Swinney

MONARCH
BOOKS

Oxford, UK & Grand Rapids, Michigan, USA

First published in the UK 2007 by Monarch Books
(a publishing imprint of Lion Hudson plc),
Wilkinson House, Jordan Hill Road, Oxford OX2 8DR.
Tel: +44 (0)1865 302750   Fax: +44 (0)1865 302757
monarch@lionhudson.com
www.lionhudson.com

ISBN: 978-1-85424-797-1 (UK)
ISBN: 978-0-8254-6150-7 (USA)

Distributed by:
UK: Marston Book Services Ltd, PO Box 269, Abingdon, Oxon OX14 4YN;
USA: Kregel Publications, PO Box 2607,Grand Rapids, Michigan 49501.

British Library Cataloguing Data
A catalogue record for this book is available from the British Library.

Printed and bound in Great Britain by Cox & Wyman Ltd, Reading.

For Shawn

Contents

Acknowledgments

*F*irst thanks belong to the couples whose stories fill these pages. I am amazed and grateful for the generosity and honesty with which they shared such personal histories. They are all, without exception, wonderful human beings: thank you each and every one.

I am deeply indebted to a great team of people who dauntlessly took up the task of reading, correcting and generally pummelling my first draft into a presentable shape in the short time I gave them to accomplish this. These saints are Miranda Harris and Becky Davies, who did a fantastic job on my last book too, Jan Palmer and Christine Daniel, women in my church who spend their time helping people with marriage matters, Lindsey Mackie, a fellow writer and friend, James Leech and Peter Harris, grammar fiends and contributors to the male perspective on this subject and Esther Youlten, my lovely sister. Thank you all!

I wrote this book in an ever-expanding body, and my intention was to complete it before my first daughter showed up. She had other plans, however, and began her (continuing) disruption of my carefully-organized life by arriving a critical ten days early. Alexa, I love you! Thank you for the wonderful chaos... you make my world a more interesting place. A big thank you is also due to the people who played with my baby and gave me windows of time to write in her first weeks of life, especially Anne French, Sarah Steel and Barbara Drewett.

Lastly, thank you Shawn for being my husband. It is fun, satisfying and occasionally crazy-making living life with you – I love it, and it just gets better and better.

Foreword

Deciding to get married is a momentous decision and, yes, some would say a crazy one at that. 'Cheerful madness' is a good way to describe it! You are choosing to spend the rest of your life with another human being; pledging to love each other and stay together through thick and thin (including, for most, thickening waist lines and thinning hair lines!); committing to support and encourage each other on the easy days, when you think the other is fabulous, and on those days when they are driving you mad.

We were married young. Thirty years on we still think marriage is a fantastic adventure, but when we looked lovingly into each other's eyes and said our vows, we could never have foreseen what was around the corner: Where our jobs would take us; whether we could have children; how we would turn out. That is the thing about the decision to marry – it involves risk, and taking a risk isn't easy, especially when it involves the rest of your life.

We live today in a risk-averse culture where we like to plan and take precautions for every eventuality. Maybe that is one of the reasons so many are hesitant about marriage. We are looking for assurances. We want to 'know' that it's right; how long we should go out together before we get engaged; how old (or young) we should be and that God is guiding us. Basically, we want a formula that will ensure we don't make a mistake. But, as Jo so compellingly shows, there is no one formula because no two couples are exactly alike.

What we need today are real life stories: stories of couples who were brave enough to take the plunge and have not regretted it; stories of how they got to the point of decision; stories of the certain and the less than certain; stories that restore our hope in marriage and help us decide whether or not to get married. And that's exactly what Jo gives us. Through her wonderful blend of realism, humour and practical advice lies a message of freedom: the freedom to make our own decision and the freedom to write our own love story.

If you are engaged, or in a relationship and wondering whether or not to get engaged, this book will help you enormously. If you are married, you will enjoy finding the story most like yours and the realization of what you have learnt along the way. If you are single and hoping one day to be married, then we would encourage you to read on: your thinking will expand and the possibilities extend.

Just one tip before we leave you to enjoy the wisdom and cheerful madness contained within these chapters. In our experience the best marriages are the ones where both partners invest in the relationship. That means discovering what makes the other feel loved; putting each other first; making time for your marriage; keeping the romance and fun alive and nurturing a healthy sex life. In other words, working at it – sometimes they fail to tell you that in the fairy stories!

Nicky and Sila Lee

Introduction

ife is full of decisions. Some are trivial and we make them quickly and easily (I will have strawberry jam on my toast this morning). Some seem obvious, and almost make themselves (I will wear my shiny black shoes to my interview today, not my wellies). Some involve an ethical or moral struggle (I'm going to hand in the wallet full of cash I just found) and some seem entirely open to personal discretion (I am going to name my child Edwina). Every now and then we are faced by a huge decision, one which will effect the whole direction our lives take from that point on. Of these kind of decisions, the decision of whom to marry is a towering giant.

Many of us girls have marriage on the brain from the moment we can form coherent thoughts. We design our wedding dresses, pick our bridesmaids and choose our colour schemes, updating them periodically as fashions change and friendships shift in focus. My first wedding dress designs had huge puffy sleeves and bustles with bows. I had a trial run in the street aged five, dragging the vicar's compliant son up the tarmacked aisle followed by my three-year-old sister, dutifully playing the bridesmaid in a strange woolly hat and a sort of sheet/dress contraption. Later on, the potential groom takes on more significance. It would break many an adolescent boy into a cold sweat if he knew how many weddings in which he had played a starring role. We try on grooms for size in an endless, secretive audition for the main part.

I suspect you boys don't give a passing thought to your future weddings until you have a fiancée who squeezes vague opinions out of you on place settings and processional music. I'm thinking you might care more about what car you'll drive when you get your license in ten years time, and how to get to the top of that bendy tree in the woods behind your house. But that's okay; we end up in the same place eventually: exchanging vows and becoming man and wife. What a miracle!

The Script

There is a scenario that I suspect lurks in the back of many of our minds, a scenario that we use as a reference point, as the normative or ideal progression. If we deviate from this perfect path, we worry that it might not be right to go ahead, that we do not have the correct feelings and details in place and we must pull out and wait until we find ourselves in a situation that does match this ephemeral prototype.

So what is the scenario? Here is my version, and maybe you could think about what yours is, if you have one.

Once upon a time, a girl met a boy. They met at university, and when they went home to meet the families, their families were very happy for them. The boy was clever, funny and handsome, and one year older than the girl. He planned to start an innovative humanitarian project in Africa when he graduated. The girl didn't know what she wanted to do, but knew she'd like to do something worthwhile in Africa and was excited that she didn't have to be innovative now she could tag along with the boy. She had lots of friends, who all thought the boy was a very good idea. After one year of spending time in groups and occasionally alone (being very well behaved of course), they both knew they were made for each other.

One day, the boy invited the girl out for a special date. They went to a posh restaurant and the girl's heart fluttered as she felt this was maybe to be the night. As they walked in the misty park after dinner, the boy got down on one knee and from his pocket produced a huge glittery diamond ring that he had chosen himself. 'I love you. Will you marry me?' he asked. 'Of course!' she replied, her heart bursting with joy.

Then they went and had champagne with the parents, who already knew the happy news since the boy had asked the girl's father for her hand in marriage.

The End

If this is uncannily like the situation you found yourself in, congratulations and I hope you have been very happy. But let's face it, there are as many different stories as there are couples, and how boring it would be if there weren't. I am writing this book out of a conviction that marriage is a GOOD thing, a gift from God that can potentially enrich our lives and refine our characters. But I sense a widespread fear and reluctance to enter into such commitment. I thought it would be encouraging to hear some of the many and varied ways that people have decided to enter this somewhat crazy institution, if only to illustrate that there is no one 'right way' to go about it. And if any of you are like me, you will enjoy a few good romantic yarns to read in the bath! These stories include an arranged marriage, a couple who were engaged within two months of meeting, a love story with plenty of tribulation and doubt along the way, a couple who started dating as teenagers, and a couple who found each other as pensioners. You may hear echoes of your own story in theirs and find their experiences comforting and validating. You may just enjoy them for their individuality and the happy outcomes (sorry – no suspense here – they all end up engaged. I can tell you that now). Along the way we will look at issues as they arise: How do we know we are doing the right thing? What parts do head and heart play in the decision-making process? How much attention do we pay to the views of our wider community? What does it mean to be compatible? How do we deal with doubts and fears? Is there such a thing as the perfect spouse out there in the world for us? Does God show us who to marry or are we on our own? I don't expect you to agree with all my conclusions (I actually don't reach many anyway) but hopefully by raising the issues it will start some helpful trains of thought. Each chapter concludes with some questions. If these are relevant to you, you might want to consider journaling your responses and then discussing them with your significant other, and possibly some other appropriate person. It could be that they help clarify your mind, or even shake up uncertainty you didn't know you had.

Before I started writing I thought I would be addressing a female-only audience, but very quickly I realized I wanted to talk to the guys as well. Since getting married, I have given myself license to take on a sort of kindly aunt role with the single men I know – which really means I ask them very personal and blunt questions about their love lives or lack of them. Men, I discover, struggle just as much, if not more, with the decisions of whether to get engaged, when to do it, who to get engaged to and how to go about it. I do know of examples of women doing the proposing, but still it is far more likely that the guy will have to do the asking, and so I hope this book will be helpful to you too.

Some of my couples appear in the pages of this book as themselves. Others have chosen to be disguised. All the stories are in their essential elements true, and all have led up the aisle and beyond, where we leave them in the assumption that they are having their ups and downs but making it work and are glad that they did it. Romance, love, life-long commitment – these things are alive and well, and I think that deserves celebrating.

1

Playing Catch-Up

t would be dignified and tidy if couples always fell for each other at precisely the same moment, if they saw each other and ZING BAM BOOM love hit them both between the eyes. More often, one person will be quite taken with the other and then have a bit of a mission to get them to reciprocate. This can involve some cunning manoeuvres: new hobbies, a haircut, financial investment in coffees, meals, gifts and plane tickets, a bit of discomfort and inconvenience as you loiter in the cold somewhere out of your way in order to 'bump into' them in the street (don't do that very often or they will get suspicious and maybe call the police) and digging out all your best anecdotes and jokes to make you appear fascinating and funny and generally irresistible. Basically, to use an old-fashioned term, you will need to 'woo' them.

If one person has been interested in the other for a lot longer, this could potentially create an awkward dynamic. Say Miss Cool has finally fallen for Mr Infatuated. Mr Infatuated might be a bit insecure for a while about whether he still cares more for her than she for him, putting her in a position of power over him. Or

Miss Cool might feel she has to make it up to him for the years she spent trying to crush his spirit and douse his ardour, and find it hard to relax and be herself. Let's see how it worked out for a real live couple.

Jess and Ben

Jessica and I are friends from boarding school days, so I have seen this story unfold over the years it has taken to come to fruition. I would never make a reliable fortune-teller because if you had asked me at any stage whether this thing was going to go anywhere but 'heartbreak city' for Jess, I would have confidently replied, 'Not a chance!' A big white wedding seemed the unlikeliest of outcomes, and I didn't want to encourage Jess in daydreams that I assumed were so far out of her reach.

Ben had been part of Jess's childhood, the son of close family friends. As the eldest in his family and the youngest in hers, they had not interacted much other than to sit in the same bathwater (I'm embellishing here, but I don't think it's beyond the realm of possibility – friends do seem to like to put their children in a bath together whenever the opportunity arises). The families liked to think that one day they would marry off their children to each other, but no one thought to pair up Ben and Jess.

Ben's family moved to Canada when he was nine and they saw little of each other until he came to England for a few months after finishing school. I stayed with them for several days in the run up to Christmas, and Jess and I talked about how pretentious he was, with his Gaulloises and philosophizing. When I saw her back at school after the holidays, we had the strangest conversation... obviously things had taken a dramatic twist.

After we had finished squealing at each other in schoolgirl fashion, I asked something normal like 'How are you?', to which she replied nonsensically, 'Ben'. Attempting to understand this strange turn in the conversation, I asked 'What, did you kill him?' It seemed like the likeliest drama to involve them both given the outlook when I had left. But what she said next was more shocking to me than homicide: 'No, I didn't kill him. I love him.' And that was that. Ben found his way into every conversation I had with Jess for the next eight years. It seemed like the crush that would not die, and honestly, I felt sorry for her and wished she would move on.

But the story is always more complicated than that; as with most crushes, there was plenty of fuel to stoke her feelings. Take for example that Christmas she first developed feelings for him. They had stayed up talking night after night once the family had gone to bed, and he made her feel special and appreciated. Although he was deliberately neglecting his appearance to make an anti-image statement, she saw beyond the big beard and horrible clothes and noticed he had lovely eyes, which looked at her intently and gave her goose bumps. When he left to go back to Canada, he gave her a card which was less than straightforward, concluding as it did, 'I cannot, nor should I, express the feelings I have for you.' What is a fifteen-year-old to make of that? Or a person of any age when it comes to that? This card stopped her sleeping for five nights in a row, and then came back to school to be analysed and treasured and stuck up on the wall above her desk to distract her. She told herself over and over again that it was not realistic to hope for anything other than friendship, and that she was crazy to have feelings for him, but who can stem the emotions of a love-struck teen, especially with the encouragement of that last ambiguous phrase on 'The Card'. Oh pleasant agony!

At half-term she sneaked into her dad's study and found Ben's contact details on his computer. Her first email took forever to craft, as she tried to capture a cool yet alluring tone, attempting to maintain the level of intimacy they had achieved in their midnight conversations while showing she was not assuming anything of their relationship. A very long week later, she received a reply: short and succinct but still enough to keep the fires of affection burning. The emails continued, as did the daydreaming. She planned how they would tell their parents, and sorted the details of their wedding – location, bridesmaids, guest list. For her he was the perfect man – sensitive, questioning, honest and of course he had those eyes...

This low-key communication and high intensity imagining continued for longer than she could comfortably tolerate, and then sometime after it ceased to be comfortable or even remotely enjoyable, she decided it had to stop. When they next saw one another Jess told him she didn't think they should correspond any longer. It was a good resolution, and she had every intention of keeping it, but it didn't hold, and they continued to write until she left school.

That summer, Jess went to Tanzania with a team of volunteers to build an orphanage. Ben happened to be in the same place leading another team, but they had no opportunity to be alone or to talk, as she so longed to do. She wondered if he was actively avoiding her. Then on the second last day, she discovered from some girls in his group that their correspondence was not unique – he was writing to at least two others in a similarly intimate and friendly manner. Ouch! She suddenly saw herself as the naïve victim of an experienced charmer, and her anger and hurt pride meant it was easy to cut contact, after she had sent as much venom through cyberspace as cyberspace could convey (enough to hit its mark, as he later told her). He was well and truly wounded.

You might think this would be the end. I certainly did, but as I said, I am not an expert in the predicting-the-future department. Somehow, they got back in touch, and her bruised feelings mended, revived and then came to the forefront once more. Due to start at Bristol University in a few short months she was determined to sort things out one way or another, and bought a ticket to Canada. 'Jess!' I cried, thinking I knew best, 'What are you doing? This is madness!'

She found herself a job and went for two months, during which time he treated her as a distant family friend. As I spoke to a tearful Jess over the phone it was all I could do not to jump on a plane and sort him out. And all I could do not to say, 'I told you so.'

Two weeks before she left they went on a walk round the neighbourhood, and Jess, with great courage, confronted him, asking him why he had been so distant. His response was that she couldn't expect the level of relationship they had developed over email. She told him what a big part of her life he had become, and then, out of the blue, he dropped a bomb shell: 'I thought I was going to marry you, but I was wrong.'

As she had done on many occasions through the years, she cried herself to sleep that night with confusion and misery inspired by this guy she couldn't seem to shake. Lying on her soggy pillow in the heavy darkness, she had the sense that it was really the end this time, and in the middle of the emptiness of this knowledge she felt God speak his love to her and knew deep down that she would be okay.

Jess still had some questions she wanted answered before leaving, not least when he had thought he was going to marry her, and why he now thought he was wrong. With these major queries in mind, she asked him to meet her for breakfast on her last Saturday in Canada. They sat in a Denny's and he ate a massive plate of food – ham, eggs, sausages, pancakes, hash browns and toast, while she sipped an orange juice. At one point she blurted out that she still loved him. Eventually, they got the bill and left, but rather than going home they drove for miles. Jess talked to him about how she saw value in a relationship that built over time, and Ben in return said he wanted something more dramatic – a sudden, instant flash of attraction and certainty. They both became more and more light-hearted and happy as the day went by, going for coffee, then to the cinema, then out to eat. When he dropped her off he told her it had been the best day of his life.

The next day he called her and asked her to meet him for coffee. No longer naïve and susceptible to charm, Jess was not inclined to accept the invitation easily: 'Why do you want to go out for coffee?'

'I want to be with you.'

'That's not helpful. Don't say things like that.'

Nevertheless, they met up and went for a walk. Jess was silent; she had nothing left to say. He, however, had plenty. Before they had gone two blocks he had told her he loved her.

As her friend this was a shocking development to absorb. I confess I had begun to think Jess was wasting her time on him some years earlier, and nothing had given me reason to hope it would work out. But it was amazing to see her return from Canada glowing with happiness and confidence, even when the pining set in and all that seemed to make her smile was the arrival of the postman.

A few months later, Ben was in England for his grandfather's funeral. While they were alone for a few hours in her parents' house, he got down on his knees and asked her to marry him. She was so fixated on the ring being proffered her, a glorious antique white gold band with what she later described as a 'big, fat diamond' (having admired the said ring myself, I can tell you the description is accurate!) that her first response was to ask if she could put it on. He wouldn't let her until he had an answer, which was a resounding yes.

Jess had her happy ending, and although she sometimes struggles still to accept he really is in love with her, I can report that they really are to all intents and purposes blissfully content together. As it worked out for her, I asked her if she would encourage others in a similar situation to hold out hope over the long haul, and patiently wait for their love to be requited. Her answer was to give a strong caution to such a person to guard their heart, and to give their feelings to God over and over again. She warned of the dangers of daydreaming and creating a person in one's mind who doesn't exist. She said you can't take hope from someone else's story, as the particularities of anyone's life are so specific and the fact that she and Ben have ended up together was the result of many unique twists and turns. She does not see the process she has been through as ideal although she is, quite obviously and rightly, pleased with the outcome.

Crushes

Crushes begin young. A child of five can turn a deep hue of red and lose the power of speech and coordination in the presence of a certain member of the opposite sex just as much as a thirteen-year-old, or let's face it, a thirty-year-old. My youngest sister Beth was part of what amounted to a harem of girlfriends when she started school aged four. Andreas was the love-god of the playground despite looking like a baby guinea pig (all head and no body), and would daily rank his female admirers according to preference. The days when she was number one or two, as opposed to say, five or six, were good days for my sister.

I had a terrible crush when I was eleven. I was not likely to feature on any love-god's girlfriend list as my popularity was on a par with our unpopular maths teacher's, but one boy in our class made the mistake of being nice to me one day. I think he said he liked my shoes (grubby yellow canvas – of course he liked them. What's not to like?). With this one innocuous comment he earned my passionate devotion for the whole academic year. Damian temporarily became the glowing centre of my small universe, lighting it up with his infrequent smiles and occasional acknowledgments of my existence. The whole thing came to a terrible denouement when, egged on by a friend, I wrote a declaration of my feelings which an intermediary gave him on the school bus, and which he proceeded to read aloud with derision before ripping it, and my heart, into small pieces.

Undeterred, I went on to have many more of these unrequited infatuations, and even became the object of undesired affections myself. While it is uncomfortable and awkward to be the admirer, it can be even more so to be the admired. I was the recipient of a note one uncomfortable day, and while I tried to be respectful and mindful of the author's feelings, I also found I had the irresistible urge to hide whenever I saw him from then on.

So what is a crush? Based on my own unfortunately extensive experience I would say it is a strong attachment to a person who may or may not be aware of who you are, in which the imagination is key and much is made of small encouragements. The person you are so devoted to may bear no actual resemblance to who they really are, and you end up giving significance to tiny interactions that might not mean a lot. They can start out giving you a sense of sparkle and excitement, but can quickly become anguished, leading you to behave irrationally and to bore your friends with incessant analysis.

There are some awkward transitions that need to happen if a crush is to turn into a realistic, mature relationship, which isn't to say it can't be done. The object of the crush must be allowed to be who they are, flaws and all, and the person with the crush must get over the feeling that the object of their admiration is somehow superior and out of reach.

Unrequited Love

Often in a relationship one person develops feelings before the other. A friend of mine, Karen, was pursued by a lovesick admirer for over three years before developing reciprocal feelings – she was just in time as the poor bloke was about to admit defeat. Falling for someone when they have not yet fallen for you does not mean the enterprise is doomed, but there are some strategies that might help along the way:

1. Stay in real life. Try to discipline yourself not to have fabricated conversations in your mind in which the object of your affections says to you, 'I have loved you since before I met you – you just couldn't tell because I was afraid of rejection and hid my feelings in a cave in Afghanistan.'

2. Get to know the person and find out who they actually are. It is easy to project qualities onto someone that you want them to have when in reality they are totally different.

3. Stay true to yourself. If the relationship is to work in the fullness of time, they must see and grow to appreciate the real you. Don't try to be the sort of person you imagine they would be attracted to: just be you. If they are not drawn to that then it would never work anyway.

4. Don't scare them. There is nothing more creepy than finding a person 'coincidentally' around every corner, remembering and quoting every minor conversation you ever had and developing an interest in pot-bellied pig rearing/antique teapots/competitive tug of

war/picture frame restoration, etc., just because you happen to do these things in your free time.

5. Don't get too excited about minor encouragements. You will know if they like you back because they will say something along those lines. Anything short of that and it doesn't add up to much.

6. Know when you're defeated and walk away with your dignity intact. Signs of ultimate defeat may include an invitation to their wedding to someone else, a restraining order, the fact that their dog bites you but is docile and sweet natured to everyone else, their sudden emigration to Australia... you get the picture (at least I hope you do).

So much for the 'don'ts'. Should you give up all hope then? I don't think so. What you can do if you are brave enough is to let them know early on of your interest. Then at least you know where you stand. Otherwise, try to get to know them in a natural way. Look at why you are interested in them and assess whether you have solid reasons. Talk to as few people as possible about it and don't let it develop into an obsession. Keep the outcome on an open palm, and pray that God will guard your heart.

The Desired Outcome

Right, so the dream has come true and the object of your private obsession has decided you are pretty hot too, and somehow things have become real and earnest. You are thinking of getting married. What are the issues particular to your situation that need to be addressed at this point? Well, I would say you need to be sure you feel respected, loved and valued, and not merely the grateful recipient of charitable regard. They are as lucky to have you as you are to have them and don't forget that. I would also say that you need to be sure you have a realistic understanding of who they are. Take a sledge hammer to the pedestal, set them down at your level and have a good long stare at what you see. This is the person who you will be living life with – can you accept them when they have stepped out of your dreams and into your car? (there are times when 80's pop says it so perfectly). Only then do a little victory dance, get out the bubbly and start planning the wedding. Congratulations my friend – you caught your prey!

Questions

1. Did you use any underhand methods to get your way? Chemicals? Voodoo? Blackmail? If so, ask yourself if you really want to be with someone who needed these sorts of encouragements to agree to marry you. Hint: you don't. Please say you don't.

2. Now you have got them do you still want them? What would a dog do if it ever caught the car it was chasing?

3. Did you have to make any radical changes to your appearance, character or circumstances to win the affection of your true love? What were they? Are you ever likely to resent them for these? You won't ever get your old nose back you know. It is gone forever. And it was a nice nose whatever she says.

2

Whirlwind Romance

hirlwind romances make great stories, and in this genre, the shorter and the more shocking the better. The most extreme example in my repertoire is my friend Erin's parents who, in a rash move completely out of character for both of them, got engaged a week after meeting. They have now been married for forty-five years. Neither of them has done anything remotely unpredictable since, but that one historical act has endowed them with an air of mystery that means nothing they could do would be truly surprising any longer.

Watching an intensely fast engagement happen is something like watching a good thriller at the cinema. You get a bit of a vicarious rush, watching someone else take the risks and getting caught up in the emotion from a safe distance while munching your popcorn, eyes jammed open in suspense. The more you care about the stars on the screen, the more you feel the fear and exhilaration of what is transpiring before you, and the more you long for a happy ending – the happy ending in this case of a long, successful and contented marriage to validate that hastily made commitment. Ken and Jen are a wonderful advertisement for this style of relationship. Allow me to introduce you.

31

Ken and Jen

Ken, webmaster extraordinaire at Regent College, Vancouver, was thirty-three, and definitely not on a wife hunt when the woman who was to change his life burst onto the scene. His anti-hunting stance was due partly to principle ('You do not shop for a spouse – they are a human being made in the image of God, not a commodity.' Yes Ken! Thank you for the lecture!) and partly self-protection. From the age of ten, Ken has been afflicted by a severe form of arthritis, ankylosing spondylitis. This is a debilitating and painful condition – although you won't hear much about the pain from Ken – which causes joints in the body to fuse together over time. He saw himself as damaged goods and assumed no woman with any other choices would choose him. And he didn't want to be with someone just because they couldn't get anyone else. So he was coasting along, enjoying life and mostly very content with his lot, aware of the pretty females streaming through the college doors but by no means burning with frustrated desire for any of them.

One day, sitting at his desk, he noticed, for the second time that week, the smell of marijuana wafting through the air. Any other location in the Pacific north-west (such as the beach, the grocery store, the gym...) and this would not be cause for comment, but in a Christian college it was unexpected, and Ken went off to investigate. Walking around the outside of the building he found two construction workers smoking over the air intake vents. Case closed. He went back inside and passed through the bookstore to explain what was going on to the staff who had noticed that the browsers in the biblical studies ection were starting to have silly smiles on their faces.

This was a good opportunity to grab a coffee (Canadians seldom pass by these opportunities). Jen was also in the line – up at the bookstore coffee shop and they began talking – first about the hot topic of the moment: the smell. This smell, for Jen, is reminiscent of bus rides to high school – the kids at the back got stoned and everyone else got munchies – just another school morning in Backwoods, USA. From pot they got on to U2. In trying to impress her, Ken let drop that he had a hard-to-come-by ticket for an upcoming concert, despite only having the one ticket and no intention of letting it out of his grasp for anyone, no matter how beautiful. Fortunately Jen didn't push the issue. From U2, via the last song on the band's *All That You Can't Leave Behind* recording, the conversation turned to the concept and reality of grace. Two hours later, Ken made it back up to his office to resume whatever tasks occupy a webmaster's workday.

Jen had arrived at Regent aged twenty-six and planning on lifelong celibacy. After two years of being housebound with sickness she had gone a bit wild and amply made up for the lost dating time. When she realized this was not how she really wanted to live her life, she broke up with the last guy she had been seeing, who it turned out had been seeing three other women at the same time and had a daughter stashed away who he'd forgotten to mention. It gets worse. In Jen's own words: 'About a month after I broke up with him he showed up at my house and, well, I spent the last three months of my time living in the US dealing with the rape crisis centre, court, lawyers and the like trying to get a protection order from him. I was rather through with men.'

After the encounter in the coffee shop, they met occasionally in passing, and had one long phone call, when Ken had found out that Jen was at home sick. Then one afternoon Jen dropped by his office to say 'hi' after a class, and he offered to give her a lift home. This was during an interminable bus strike, which was of no benefit to anyone except Ken at this particular moment, who was afforded a prime opportunity to make some progress with his attempts to get to know Jen. On the way home, she told him she felt safe with him, a weighty compliment given her recent history.

A beady-eyed female colleague cornered Ken shortly afterwards, having spotted them leaving the building together, and wanted to know what was going on (he insists that she was a good friend and had earned the right to ask such personal questions). He evaded the question, friendship notwithstanding, and she bluntly told him that there was something going on even if he was too slow to pick up on it, and he should take action. Men sometimes need friends like that!

The next night, Ken had invited Jen to join him and some others at the Cheshire Cheese, a Vancouver bar trying very hard to be an 'olde worlde' English pub. When he went to collect her, the following, now legendary, exchange took place:

Ken: Jen, I think I'm having a hard time not falling for you.
Jen: Well, don't let me stop you.

Before we go on, let's take a quick look at the time line of this relationship. First meeting – 1 February. The Cheshire Cheese conversation – 23 February. Official engagement – 5 May. Marriage ceremony – 18 August. And all this in the same year! These guys did not waste time.

So what happened in the two short months between their declaration of interest and their engagement? Ken maintains that he was not swept up in the madness of romantic love, (although I have to say, as an objective observer, he did have plenty of symptoms of the most severe kind of lovesickness), but was rather complying with the inevitable, something powerful and beyond his control. As he puts it, 'It may sound strange, but I still don't feel like I "decided" to marry Jen. In many ways I felt the decision had already been made for me, and I was just going along, albeit perfectly willingly.' I can just hear the jealous gnashing of teeth as you start your twenty-fifth pros and cons list and hurl your magic eight ball out of the window. Yep, some people have it easy.

When it came to meeting each other's families, Jen had the daunting task of impressing not only Ken's parents, but also his SEVEN brothers! This she accomplished with finesse, and he likewise managed to win wholehearted approval from her more conventionally-sized family. By the middle of April, Ken had asked Jen's father for permission to marry her, and Jen had bought piles of bridal magazines and had started planning the wedding with her mother.

By this point, Ken, Jen and most of their family and friends knew they were going to get married. All that remained was to stage a dramatic proposal – a bit of a challenge given that the surprise factor was going to be rather limited. Ken found a ring and carefully planned a day out that would take them round all of Vancouver's most romantic hotspots, at each of which he would NOT propose (there's that sneaky surprise factor we were missing!), culminating with a big party back at his house, where he would finally ask her to marry him. The day before the plan was to take place, Jen's doctor had found some significant lumps in her breast. She was nervous and anxious and was told to stop drinking coffee immediately: the appointment was early and she had not even had her first cup of the day. Serious coffee drinkers will know how bad she felt about that, especially when I tell you it was a false alarm and the embargo was all for nothing. Here is her account of the next day:

> We went to one of our usual Saturday morning breakfast places where the Aussie waiter met us with the greeting, 'Yahtzee!' because we always played on the pocket pc while we waited to eat... and I lost MISERABLY. And no coffee. Then we went to some private school garage sale (and we got there late so there wasn't much to see). Then to Queen Elizabeth park where I wanted to steal flowers and then to the conservatory, both places full of bridal parties having pictures taken, very romantic, no Big Question. We ended up getting a couple of chocolate bars to see if my coffee headache would go away (it didn't). And then we went to Granville Island to pick up stuff for dinner and Ken bought me a full-caffeine coffee because he didn't want to risk me saying no because I had a headache. I remember thinking he was a special guy because he was buying champagne for dinner, and I'd long given up on the proposal.

Ken takes up the story:

> After a full day we drove back to my house. As we got out of the car I told Jen to look at the beautiful garden my landlords had tended oh so well. She seemed to

find this a little odd as she had seen and admired it many times before. At that moment a few of my brothers and some friends came up from behind the house singing 'I Can't Help Falling in Love with You' by Elvis and I got down on one knee and pulled out the ring. I asked, 'Jen, will you marry me?' to which she responded, 'What do you think?' which, as it turns out, was a yes.

Ken and Jen have remained beautifully and blissfully happy to this day – their relationship seems truly blessed. In the midst of this marital glow they have horrible health problems to deal with and have discovered that they may not be able to have their own children, so let's not begrudge them the gift of each other. Not that life is fair anyway (bad marriage = good health, good health = no money, no money = good looks... that would be fair right? How come some people get all or none? That's a perplexing question). Suffice to say, I am glad Ken and Jen have each other – no two people deserve a happy marriage more.

Speed and Substance

If there was any overarching message I intended to convey through the stories told in this book, it would be that all our stories are unique. No formula can guarantee the right decision being made. To choose a marriage partner is one of the greatest challenges we will face in life, and will have enormous impact on all other facets of our existence – there is no wriggling out of our own responsibility in making this decision. We can follow general wisdom, specific advice and our inner voice (if we can hear it above the din of all that wisdom and advice), and then we must live with our choice. So I will not lay down any approved time lines or infallible rules of thumb, but rather share some thoughts that may or may not be helpful to you in your situation.

It strikes me that a speedy engagement is sometimes a good idea and sometimes not, depending mostly on the reasons for the speed. When is it a good idea? Well, in our culture, where commitment is feared and often avoided, a man and woman who are willing to give themselves to a lifelong exclusive relationship are to be commended, as long as they fully know and understand that this is what they are indeed embarking upon. If a couple waits five or ten years before addressing the long-term implications of their relationship, they might have grown accustomed to living in a house with open doors and find the thought of shutting themselves in a bit claustrophobic. If the individuals know in principle that they want to be married, and then meet each other and realize they want to be married specifically to that person, then there is no good reason to spin out the process. For some people, it is a natural and straightforward thing to decide a course of action and then follow it through. Leaving the decision open-ended for a year simply to appease convention would not make any difference to the quality of their commitment. Self-knowledge is extremely important at this point. Are you the sort of person who can stick with a decision, or do you feel passionately in the moment and then feel just as passionately later that the opposite position would be the right one?

I do think that the age and stage of life you are at is pertinent here. Ken and Jen had lived enough to know what they wanted and didn't want from life and from a spouse. They had made plenty of important decisions, such as where to live and what to do, and knew what a bad decision entailed as well as a good one. A fast engagement for a very young person is far scarier for the observer, as so much still lies ahead, and so much could change. You have to ask why the rush?

Sometimes circumstances might force a decision to be made faster than it would have been. I have known couples to get engaged on the diagnosis of a terminal illness – not only does time become very precious in this situation, but it seems to clarify which doubts are important and which are frivolous. On a practical level, it means that the healthy person becomes a next of kin and can be far more involved in treatment and in supporting their loved one in hospital, and emotionally, it gives them a greater unity and intimacy as they face the pain and likely bereavement. Other circumstances that can expedite an engagement are life changes that need to take into account whether the relationship is a permanent fixture or not, such as a move abroad, the purchase of a house or a vocational upheaval. If life throws up such challenges, there is not much to do but make the best decision you can, and quite likely it will be as good a decision as the one you would have made three years later anyway.

Bad Reasons for a Quick Engagement

Sometimes we make very bad decisions for very bad reasons and things work out just fine. But it is generally a good idea to try not to. With this in mind, here are some suggestions of unhealthy reasons for a premature diamond purchase:

- Diamonds are on sale at Wal-Mart and the offer ends on Tuesday. So what if you just met two weeks ago? Prices could never be this low again.
- I must have sex or I will explode, and I will only have sex within marriage. Better to marry than to burn with lust, right St Paul?
- My parents don't like him, and I like anything my parents don't like. This will really get them mad!
- She lives in Mexico and it hasn't stopped raining in Mudditon-Under-Vale for two years. I can't take another day of this: she could be my ticket to a new, sunnier life.
- My last boyfriend broke my heart. Let's see how he feels when he finds out I got married seven weeks after he left me – HA.
- His visa runs out in fifty-two hours. He could stay if he was my fiancé.
- She's so pretty. I feel fluffy when I'm with her. Can't think straight. Can't sleep. Can't eat. Did I mention how pretty she is?
- I must have some drama in my life. Things are getting boring round here. I have shaved my head, streaked at Wimbledon, painted the front of my house purple and orange, adopted an abused llama, started a few small-ish fires… I know, I'll propose to my girlfriend in record time!
- Two words: Babies, Menopause.

There are times when you might slow things down against your natural inclinations. Let me share briefly how this worked for me and Shawn here. We had both seriously considered marriage with other people in the past, and from these experiences knew that we wanted to get married, but not to any of the options we had so far been presented with. In the first few weeks of knowing each other we had a strong sense that 'this was it' and things were going to work out for us. We had a couple of tentative conversations along these lines, and then decided it would be sensible to wait awhile before formalizing anything as we knew our backgrounds and cultures were worlds apart and that we would have plenty of reassuring to do as far as friends and family went. So to cut a short story shorter, we got engaged after seven months of dating. Ken and Jen wrote tauntingly in our engagement card, 'What kept you, slow pokes?' Some people wait until the completion of their studies. Other reasons to wait might include fulfilling a work contract, or being under the age of sixteen (in some countries anyway). Waiting can be the most sensible thing to do, even if it is frustrating.

The Head and Heart in Dialogue

Ken and Jen both felt that they did not have a decision to make – they were simply going along with things as they were preordained. They are very fortunate. For most of us, there is a combination of factors playing into the eventual outcome. One of these is emotion. When you fall in love with someone, your emotions can be very overwhelming and threaten to dominate your reason. We don't always fall in love with people who make very good marriage prospects, and yet our emotions might override any attempts to reason with ourselves. However, it can be essential to have a bit of love madness running around our bodies to help push us into what is a bit of a nutty proposition (for better for worse, till death do us part –

HEEEEELPPPP!). Ideally, both heads and hearts play their part in helping us decide what to do, and hopefully don't contradict each other too badly, as in the following scenarios:

Head: He has a good job, he treats me very well, and we have many common interests.

Heart: I never miss a beat when he comes in the room.

Head: My family like him. He is very well mannered. He has great bone structure.

Heart: I just keep beating away: ba-boom, ba-boom, ba-boom.

Head: He'd be a responsible father. He's good with money. What if I don't get any better options?

Heart: I don't want him – he's just not doing it for me. I WON'T AGREE TO THIS!

Or...

Head: She's got nothing to say.

Heart: Mmmmm – she's so snuggly. I love her.

Head: You'll get bored in a few weeks.

Heart: Marry her you fool. I want her now.

Head: You'll regret this...

Heart: I don't care. I love her. Look at her cute dimples.

Hopefully head and heart cooperate with one another, and together help us know what to do. Some of us will trust our rational minds far more and will need to be at peace with the logical basis for going ahead with marriage – compatibility, stable finances, mutual respect and so on. Others of us will be relying on our feelings to reassure us that we should be with this person. It is probably wise to pay attention to both, and if they are in severe disagreement with each other, to try and hold crisis talks and come to a resolution before taking the binding vows.

Questions

If you have time while you rush along planning your future at supersonic speed, take a moment to think about these questions:

1. What is your head saying about this decision? What is your heart saying? If you are the sort of person who enjoys a bit of creativity (silliness?), write out the conversation they would have about what to do.
2. What's the big hurry? Take a long look at your reasons for getting engaged this fast. Do they bear scrutiny?
3. What is your track record with decision making? How do you usually go about making big decisions? What major choices have you faced in your life so far, and have you been satisfied with what you decided?
4. Do your friends and family seem terrified or pleased when you tell them what you are thinking of doing?
5. Do their reactions correspond to what they did them-selves (the same or the opposite)? Do you like and admire the way their marriage is playing out? Why? Why not?

3

Rocky Road

I felt it was really important to include a couple in this discussion who found it very difficult to know whether they should get married, who didn't 'just know', who had doubts and fears and questions, yet still went ahead, and have not lived to regret the decision. I do know a few couples who would fall into this category, but as you can imagine, it is not an easy task to approach people to be this kind of case study ('Er, you know you had a horrible relationship to begin with... well, could I use you in my book to encourage other people who are also not doing so great?'). It seems, and I do understand this, that there is a temptation to retell the story once safely bound together for life in law and before God, and to sanitize some of the more traumatic twists and turns they went through on the way. So, I was extremely relieved when Jan, a member of my church, actually volunteered herself and her husband Gary for this chapter, and even more so when I realized how frank she was willing to be about what it was actually like for them as a couple whose path to marriage ran less than smoothly. The stories we tend to hear more of are the ones in which two individuals meet and are drawn inevitably and peacefully towards the logical conclusion of matrimony. This perpetuates an unhelpful myth that casts a shadow of inadequacy over the far more common experience of those who stumble about a bit, tripping over their doubts and short-sightedly feeling their way as best they can. Both scenarios can lead to equally successful and happy marriages, as this particular story illustrates.

Jan and Gary

Jan is a tall, willowy blonde, with a wave in her hair that adds to the impression of height when you first meet her. This is not a short lady, even seen from a distance with squinty eyes. I am not being facetious here – this is actually a key detail of the story. From a young age, Jan's primary criterion for her future husband was that he should match or exceed her vertical inches. Issue number one for Gary and Jan was not going to be resolved without lopping off a three-inch section of her legs or buying him some Tom Cruise-style built-up shoes, which no self-respecting rugby-playing albeit slightly short manly man would tolerate. I start with the most superficial of problems perhaps, but these things can seem intensely important.

Let's back up a bit. Sometimes the things that matter when considering marriage with someone don't even feature as a problem in the early days when it is all about having fun and enjoying the present moment, and this was the case here. Our couple first met as fellow computer programmers in 1983. It is not out of the question that when they first laid eyes on each other she was wearing shoulder pads and a patent leather belt and he was wearing an oversized blazer with the sleeves pushed up. I am not saying this was what they were wearing – just that it might be a reasonable guess. A friendship developed between them, which had opportunity to become something altogether more intimate at an alcohol-fuelled office toga party. This was the occasion of Gary's first proposal of marriage to Jan. His suit was unsuccessful, but he dealt with his devastation as best he could and went on to propose, equally unsuccessfully, to several other women that night. One can only imagine the tension around the water cooler in the office the next day.

One month later and they had their first date, in the Crooked Billet at Iver (in case this is not self-evident, the Crooked Billet is a pub, and Iver is a place where there happens to be a pub called the Crooked Billet). Those three inches aside, Jan was impressed. He was sensitive, caring and funny, and humour covers a multitude of sins, as many funny and otherwise unappealing men the world over will gratefully acknowledge. That first date led on to a four year dating relationship.

But Jan had more than the matter of the missing inches preventing her from seeing her boyfriend as husband material. Issue number two: she had a strong faith and it was important to her that she should be able to share this with a future life partner. Gary was more comfortable on the rugby pitch than in a church, and resented having to compete with the endless commitments to house group, worship leading and youth events. He took on her Christian belief as a challenge, determined to destroy it and have her for himself.

In some ways, the faith issue was a convenient way for Jan to keep Gary at arm's length. While she assumed she would get married one day, it wasn't a terribly thrilling prospect for her, largely because of the way she had seen it working out for her family and friends. There had been examples of dominant husbands and cowed wives, and the devastation experienced by a close male relative whose wife walked away with his one-year-old child. So there was the third issue: she had real doubts about marriage as a concept, let alone with a short atheist.

Gary persevered however, doggedly using any and every opportunity to ask her to be his wife, including over a Big Mac in McDonald's (Was he surprised when this didn't get the desired response, I wonder?), and getting consistently rebuffed. They would periodically break up, usually at 5.30 p.m. on a Sunday evening as she got ready for church. She would arrive at the service red-eyed and miserable and be congratulated on her wise decision by her well-meaning Christian friends, but inevitably the split would be short lived.

Eventually, Gary agreed to go to church with her. As Jan's friends there had been systematically trying to help her cut him out of her life, he understandably wanted to find a new one, so together, they searched out a new church community. Over time, Gary began to get to know God, eventually deciding to commit his life to following Him. With his new found faith, one of Jan's key issues had been resolved, and we might be forgiven for assuming sunny days lay ahead. However, a quick scan of her list of pros and cons written at that time shows that if anything, her thinking had become even more muddled and tortuous:

Pros	Cons
Companionship/ friendship	Unable to release my emotions
Support	Convincing myself it will never work
Humour	
Faith	Feelings of dread
Compatibility	Loss of independence
	Fear that we'll cease to make an effort for one another
He can do DIY and cook	Faith in my commitment is weak

Finally, after proposal number eighty-seven or thereabouts, Gary to his amazement heard her utter the miraculously ambiguous word, 'Probably'. This was not the conclusive 'No' he had been accustomed to hearing, and he grasped it as the most positive answer he was ever likely to receive. The next day they bought a ring, a Ceylon sapphire with diamonds either side, and the date was set.

For a lot of people, the commitment of engagement brings a degree of peace: the decision has been made and they can relax into a new, more settled phase of the relationship. This was not the case for Jan, whose anxieties only geared up a notch. An extract from her diary two weeks before the wedding reads:

Why this inner turmoil and panic Lord? Do you really think that I am strong enough to take this, because I am getting weak and breaking up inside. The pressure of all this uncertainty is hurting me and making me miserable. That big question of 'Am I doing the right thing?' never seems to leave me. As the days go by I get less and less confident, or is it just more and more nervous?

I know that all the arrangements would not have gone so well if it hadn't been meant. That I have sold my house and burnt my bridges is positive – no matter how much it hurts. That you have brought Gary to trust in you has made a difference. Please bring me to have that same trust. I want to be a radiant bride, wanting my husband for myself, loving him with all my heart. Whilst I am not though, can I count on Gary's view of my love being sufficient, that it is purely my emotions that are dominating me at the moment and not that love has disappeared? I have no excitement, no dreams, no urges – just blank. Is this normal, adequate to base a life together on? Please God, give me a positive attitude and spirit of acceptance rather than this fighting turmoil and conflict.

She would wake up daily with a tight knot in her stomach, wondering, 'How do you KNOW? This is forever, and how can I be sure?' She was tormented by thoughts of how she imagined she should be feeling – happy, light-spirited and positive – and knew her state of mind stood in stark contrast to anything like it. Like me, you may now have a wide-eyed admiration for Gary's confidence and loyalty, as it seems his own conviction that they were supposed to be together never wavered, even as he waited at the end of the aisle, wondering if his bride would show up. As Jan looks back and ponders the way events unfolded, she credits much of the fact that they actually got married to the way Gary handled her emotional upheaval and terror in the lead up to the wedding. He was unfailingly optimistic, consistently supportive and reassuring, listening to her and praying for her, all of which provided a solid emotional foundation for the years to come.

Well, she didn't leave him bereft at the altar, and judging by the photographs at least, was every bit the radiant bride she longed to be on her wedding day. She was still terrified walking into the church, still anxious as she said her vows and still uneasy as the honeymoon progressed. But as daily life unfolded she realized she was okay, she was going to live, and life was better with Gary than without him. Now, seventeen years and three children later, she sits across from me nursing a cup of tea, and tells me he is a thousand times more than the man she married and she has the glow of a woman happily and contentedly in love. They both see their fragile beginnings as a strength; rather than starting out feeling they had it all together and then gradually becoming disillusioned, they have been finding more and more joy in their relationship.

Comparing Notes

If you are in a bumpy, difficult relationship and trying to figure out where to go with it, you are quite possibly scooting round gathering up accounts of other people's experiences and analysing them in depth for similarities and differences to your own. You want to know if what you feel is normal, if there is a typical outcome you could expect given the facts – some sort of formula to use as a guide. This can be helpful to an extent. You may be greatly relieved to find that, although you thought there was really only one way to feel if you were ready to get engaged (completely sure) there are actually many people who get engaged without that completely sure feeling you feared was compulsory.

I suspect that the more stories you gather for your collection, the more you will discover that everyone has a completely unique tale to tell. And this is where you must be careful, because however similar you feel your relationship is to someone else's, you cannot steal their ending – you must make your own. Jan walked up the aisle on her wedding day still freaking out inside and went on to be very happily married, but the reasons for her freak-out are specific to her, and if you do the same it could be that you are making a huge mistake. So by all means draw comfort and wisdom from others around you, but don't assume you can superimpose yourself onto their narrative and thus avoid the tough decisions only you can make.

Outcomes

Last year I did one of those Myers-Briggs personality tests. I have done unofficial ones before but this was the real deal, so now I am officially boxed into a type. Actually, I reckon if I did it every few months the results would always be a bit different, because I am a very complex and completely uncategorizable person (Oh dear – that is just the sort of thing someone of my type *would* say). One bit that was definitely spot-on though, and no doubt would be consistent however often I took the test, was the bit that tells you if you prefer things open-ended or decided. I am prepared to admit that I am much happier once a decision has been made. It means that I am not the spontaneous, happy-go-lucky kind of person that I might have liked to think I was, but hey, the world needs its controlling, uptight planners right? Just don't make me go on another camper van trip round Europe with no fixed schedule, Shawn – it stressed me out! The way this relates to relationships is that I always found it very hard not knowing from the word go whether the boyfriend was going to become a husband or an ex, and would usually jump the gun far too early just to get to a conclusion faster. It goes against my character to say this, but I would advise against following my example. It is possible you will marry this person, and it is possible you will break up. Try to sit in the tension for as long as you need to in order to make the best decision, however uncomfortable it makes you. It would be equally tragic to break up with someone you could make a happy life with as to marry someone who is going to be blight on the rest of your days. Entering a new relationship is always a risk. You are strapping yourself in for a ride that is going to last an awful long time or end in a big, disastrous crash. Either way, the outcome is scary, but what would life be like without the adrenaline rush, the heightened emotions, the intensity and noise and chaos of relationships?

Get Out Now!

There are good and bad reasons for staying in a tricky relationship and trying to make it work. The good reasons would be that the trickiness is resolvable and maybe not even related to the person you are dating but to yourself. More on that later. The bad reasons may be surmountable, and plenty of people do get married from less than ideal motivations, but if you haven't yet said your vows and you find you are arguing to yourself that you should stay together for the following reasons, may I respectfully suggest they are not very good and you need to find better ones as a matter of urgency?

- 'I don't want to be alone.'
- 'I might never meet someone better.'
- 'He says God told him to marry me.'
- 'We have a holiday booked. It's non-refundable.'
- 'He says I have to marry him. I have no choice.'
- 'I have bought my wedding dress.'
- 'He is rich and I like the standard of living he is offering me.' (Plenty of Jane Austen's characters would find that a perfectly adequate basis for a marriage. Personally, I think if it stands as the only foundation for your forthcoming nuptials, the house of love will tumble down around you and your snazzy designer decor.)
- 'His parents really like me. It would upset them if we broke up.'
- 'I don't want to hurt him.'

Quick note on that last one: when I ended my two most serious relationships, I agonized over the pain I assumed I would be inflicting – it really made me feel awful. Until six weeks later when they started dating other people. I'm glad they were able to get over me, but it was quite insulting how fast this recovery appeared to kick in. Humph. So don't stay together to protect the other person. It won't be the end of everything good in their life, and if they knew you were with them just out of pity they would probably end the relationship themselves, given a certain level of self-respect.

Feel the Fear

Almost everyone has to plough through a degree of fear and doubt when deciding to marry someone. The question is, what sort of doubts are enough to stop you going ahead? Which fears are actually telling you something important that you need to pay attention to? This process of introspection is extremely challenging, and can be almost paralysing. If you think too much about something you can completely lose perspective and become confused and unsure of yourself. But it is also very necessary work, and if you can go through the middle of the doubt, you could be blessed with a satisfying and good lifelong relationship. Conversely, you could be saved from a disastrously difficult lifelong relationship or even a divorce. What is dangerous is to avoid the hard work of figuring out what is what and forcing yourself to march on towards matrimony regardless of how you feel about it. Feeling fear and doubt is not necessarily a sign that you are with the wrong person. But it could be. And you must figure out what these fears are exactly. So here are some suggestions of sources of fear that don't categorically spell disaster for your relationship:

- *Marriage as a concept scares you because your parents divorced/your best friend is in a horrible marriage/you have never seen it really work out.*

  If you can work through this fear, all the better. Look for examples of happy marriages – turn to fiction or to history if you have to. Try to analyse why the marriages you have known to fail broke down and learn from them. Weed out untrue maxims for life that you have adopted by observing the misfortunes of others and live by more optimistic principles. Take control – you, by your actions, your attitudes and your will power, have a say over the success of your marriage.

- *You were really hurt by your previous boyfriend who was unfaithful to you and you find it hard to trust that it won't happen again.*

Take the time you need to be angry, forgive and heal, and don't allow his behaviour to poison the rest of your life. This was a horrible and wrong thing to have happen to you, but you don't need to let it turn you into an indestructible turtle-like shelled creature.

- *You have always had an ideal person in your mind, and maybe they are still out there. What would you do if you met them when you were already married to the very human person you have in front of you now? Should you hold out and wait a bit longer for them to show up?*

Nah. Don't hold out. What I recommend is that you take your fantasy person into a deserted back alley and sock them over the head with something heavy like a crowbar, then hold a funeral, be a bit sad for a week, and get over them. They don't exist. They are never going to show up. Sorry.

- *You have been feeling pretty down for a few months – just not quite yourself. Maybe you would be happier if you did something drastic and ended your relationship. Then you could move to Hawaii and start over.*

It is never a good idea to make a drastic decision of any kind when you are depressed; making one radical change rarely sorts out how you feel. It could be that your relationship is the crux of your distress, but it's unlikely. And unfortunately, a change in location probably won't do the trick either: you will feel the same in Hawaii as you did in Hammersmith. Take some steps to deal with the depression, and when you are in a better state you will probably have a truer perspective on the marriage issue.

- *You feel you don't deserve to be with someone who treats you so well. Someone or something has shaken your self-esteem to the point where you scupper your chances to be happy because you don't feel worthy.*

Two words: GET COUNSELLING. Everyone deserves to be loved and to be happy – including you. Find out why you don't think you do and sort it out.

- *You like low-budget art films and your boyfriend likes Hollywood blockbusters. Oh no – How can we possibly be together under these circumstances? (This is one of the biggest obstacles that Shawn and I had to overcome. Take heart, it is surmountable.)*

It is okay to have differences. You are not going to do everything together all the time, and you don't have to like all the same things.

There are some essential things that must be in place for a marriage to work. These essentials are going to be different for each couple. My list got more and more condensed over time until I ended up with just four items: they had to be a Christian, I had to find them attractive, I had to respect their intelligence and we had to share a sense of humour. Most of all, I wanted to feel that we somehow fitted together. The reason that I don't think any of the possible sources of fear and doubt listed above are too drastic to overcome is that they either relate to superficialities of difference that will be found between any two humans, or that they relate to issues inside you and not inside the relationship. It might be that you need to slow things down and resolve some of your personal tangles before you're ready to take public vows of commitment, but it doesn't mean you are not supposed to be with your current boyfriend and that things would be any different with someone else. Or it may be that your healing will come in and through making that commitment.

Questions

It can be scary to look honestly at doubts if one of the possible outcomes is that you have to walk away. And if you are not yet married, you have to face up to the fact that this might well happen. These questions are not going to make it all suddenly clear, but they might help you through the process of discernment:

1. Does your relationship energize you or drain you overall?
2. Do you feel you are more or less yourself when you are with this person? Which positive qualities in you do they draw out? In what ways do they encourage your spiritual and emotional growth?

3. Who among your friends and family support your relationship? Who don't? What reservations have they expressed, if any, and do you feel they were justified?
4. What reasons do you have to trust this person? Have they been faithful to you? Have they told you the truth about important matters? Is their behaviour consistent and do they treat you well?
5. Do you want to be with this person? Do you like them? This may seem an obvious question, but faced with the prospect of FOREVER it can be overlooked.
6. Are you motivated to work through your difficulties? Do you deep down want things to work out between you? If so, why?
7. Is there any pattern to your previous break ups? What issues have previous heartbreaks left you with? How can you address any hurt you still carry with you?
8. How is your partner responding to your feelings of doubt?

4

A Divine Idea

*D*oes God decide who we marry? This is part of a wider debate that can easily get caught up with weighty philosophical and theological debris such as predestination, free will, the sovereignty of God, theodicy (the exercise of proving God's goodness in a world full of badness) and other flotsam and jetsam. So let's cling to a tree and watch the floodwaters rush by carrying all these gnarly issues and just pay attention to a single story. I am not using this story as a microcosm of my theology on the subject; it is simply the account of how two people experienced God's hand on their lives. In God's wonderful way, it is particular to them and exactly what was needed to bring them together.

Colin and Roni

Colin is my honorary older brother. He lived with my family in Portugal for a number of years during my childhood, while working at the field study centre we lived in. He ably filled the older brother role by beating me up, teasing me about boys, giving plenty of sought after and occasionally totally unwanted advice and by his exuberant and affectionate presence on holidays, Christmases, birthdays and all significant family events. Colin's parents are English by origin, but he was born and raised in Kenya. This partially explains his slightly unusual attire. On an average day his feet are shod in flip-flops made of car tyres – if it is cold he may wear socks as well, but mostly just the flip-flops. Around his neck will be a kikoi, a large piece of colourful fabric, which he will also use to sleep in, whip the backs of your legs, dry himself after swimming and for multiple other uses as the occasion demands. His language is peppered with Swahili and he will happily tell you that he got the scar on his misshapen collar bone when he was trodden on by an elephant.

As his adopted younger sister, I took great interest in his interactions with girls over the years. As time and a small but steady stream of beautiful, eligible women passed by, I wondered if Col would ever manage to sort himself out. It turned out that he didn't – but God certainly did.

This story is much more interesting from Roni's perspective. Col's version is that he met this fantastic, stunningly attractive lady, and after about a month decided he wanted to marry her. All well and good, but wait until you hear what else was involved in getting these two together – talk about spectacular heavenly fireworks!

Roni comes from a family of happy marriages, and from the age of about twenty, she longed to be married herself. By the time she and Col got married she was thirty-two, so this was a long time of longing and waiting and hoping.

During her second year of university in her home

country of South Africa, Roni's eye was caught by a fellow zoology student, and this initial attraction rapidly became a full blown crush. This was the first time she had ever fallen for someone in this way and she remembers it as AGONY. Somehow, she kept her feelings between her and God, who she talked to about it a *lot*, praying and journaling and stewing about the situation, but never mentioning it to her friends let alone the guy in question. After a year of this, she began to need to know if he was the one for her. She told a couple of close friends, asking them to pray about it, and approached God with a determination to hear his verdict on the matter. God did not leave her hanging. As she prayed, images came to mind which she drew in her journal. She described them to me as follows:

> The first was one of Jesus and I standing together. He was holding a huge red jewel in his hand, and the jewel seemed to represent the answer I was wanting for my future about a marriage partner. The next picture I saw was of him handing it to me. The moment I got hold of it I went running away at a pace with it firmly tucked under my arm. I drew the picture of the Lord standing in the dust as I rushed off with a thrilled expression on my face, clutching the huge jewel. I felt God ask me if there was anything wrong with this picture: yes God, I've left you in the dust! Then in the third scene, he took the big red jewel and put it in the middle of his chest. He explained that if I was to know his plans for my life, I would have to stick close to him. I saw myself giving him a big hug to be close to his purposes for my life.

The friends who had been praying for her came back and said in essence the very same thing; not yes, not no, but stick close to God and he'll show you. By the beginning of the next year, the crush had fizzled, and the wait for a husband continued. One of the consequences (and perhaps a cause?) of having to wait so long was that her list of requirements for her future husband became more and more complex and detailed. At the top of the list were the non-negotiables: he must be a sold-out-for-God Christian, and he must have a career in the bush. After this came some more general qualities, such as kindness, honesty, integrity and a sense of humour. And then she got really picky, specifying eye colour, cultural background and even parents' profession (game farmers in Botswana, or, at a push, Zambia).

Right, you need to concentrate for this bit, as I try to relate as simply as I can how Col and Roni's paths began to meander towards each other until they met several years later in Nairobi. Roni's godmother, Jacqui, has two children, a son called Roger, and a daughter called Shan. Roger met Col's younger brother in Amsterdam working with 'Youth With a Mission'. They became friends, and did a massive safari through Kenya. Some years later, Shan and her husband were planning to move to Mozambique to work as missionary teachers, and Roger suggested they go and speak to Col's parents who had worked with the same organization in Kenya for many years. Following okay so far? As they were sitting having tea, Col's mother mentioned an embarrassing moment she had had recently when her son, a mad bird watcher from Kenya, had shown up at a cousin's smart function wearing shorts and yes, you guessed it, those car-tyre flip-flops! In an instant, Shan had a shocking revelation:

this was the guy for Roni. It was a strong, clear thought and it refused to go away, only growing stronger over the following years when it seemed more and more unlikely that they would ever even meet. She had concluded that if it was of God, he would bring it about, and she did nothing to engineer fate or hurry the process in any way. Well, she did nothing except talk to her mother about it when she couldn't hold it in any longer. As Roni's god-mother, Jacqui had been eager to see her sorted out with a fine husband, and couldn't help sending out subtle hints directing her attention towards Col's existence. One of these 'subtle hints' was to send her a copy of a book about 'A Rocha', featuring, as she wrote in her card, 'a very lovely guy, Colin'. Roni did a calculation of his age, and realizing he was six years her senior, wrote him off immediately: her list specified a man of her own age, so that is what she expected God to provide.

Meanwhile, another strange thread was woven into the story. Roni's sister and brother-in-law went to Prague for a year and ended up teaching in a school set up by Col's brother and his wife. The families speculated about how well suited their siblings would be, but didn't manage to contrive a meeting.

Roni spent Christmas in Prague shortly before her sister was due to head home to South Africa. The furthest north she had been in her life prior to this was Malawi, so the ancient, snowy city blew her mind. One day they were meandering up the hill towards the castle, and ducked into a tiny, medieval-looking jewellery shop full of individually-designed bracelets and necklaces made from brass medallions. Suddenly, she caught sight of one in particular which took her breath away: it was an exact representation of the picture God had shown her six years before after praying for a husband. There was an image of Jesus as a rugged shepherd with a staff in one hand. In the crook of his arm nestled a woman, looking up at him with love and trust, and in Jesus' chest was a large red jewel. Underneath were the words, 'Christus Deo Rosha'. She bought it immediately, and kept it with her in a wooden box for the next five years, as a tangible reminder of God's faithfulness, and of her trust that he would bring her a man one day.

Much of those five years was spent in the remote South African bush, just below the Mozambique border. When the contract ended, she spent a few weeks in Durban wondering what should come next. She had an email from Shan suggesting she check out A Rocha, Kenya, and the words 'A Rocha' jumped out at her as being very similar to the words on the medallion (both 'Rosha' and 'Rocha' mean 'rock'). Then came another email, this time from Colin's mother, with details of the 'A Rocha, Kenya' website. It seemed everyone was on her case. She plucked up her courage, and after many redrafts, eventually sent her first communication to the famous Colin, an email asking if there were any jobs available. His reply a few days later was an unambiguous 'no'. There were no jobs; they were a volunteer outfit.

Shortly after this unpromising exchange, a job in Namibia came up, and Roni decided to take it, trusting God that somehow he would be able to sort her out with a husband even if she was buried in the exact middle of nowhere, wrinkling up under the harsh desert sun. Well into the full swing of the job, she was invited by her friend Sandy to go and see the wildebeest migration from Tanzania into the Maasai Mara in Kenya. She couldn't resist, and they made plans for the trip. A few weeks before she left, her ever-persistent godmother asked her, 'So when are you going to get to Kenya, Roni? Really, you MUST meet this guy!' All attempts at subtlety had long gone out of the window by this point, and Jacqui and her husband had determined to buy her air ticket if necessary – whatever it would take to make the introduction happen, they would do. As you can imagine, they were delighted to hear that she had already arranged a visit to Kenya.

After some convoluted arrangements by text, Col and Roni's first meeting was finally organized, in a narrow window of time when they would both be in Nairobi. Colin approached this meeting thinking he was to be chatting with a guy, Ronnie, who was interested in working with his organization. Roni was coming to it with years of hints and suggestions about this man being her ideal match. It must have been a fun occasion for Sandy, who had been primed as to the potential significance of the event.

After the encounter, impressions were varied:

Colin: A bit overwhelmed by two random, nutty South African girls who didn't let him get a word in edgeways and didn't seem to want to talk about A Rocha much.

Sandy: He is PERFECT for Roni! Hooray!

Roni: No way! He has a British accent, and British people spend their time vacuuming dead leaves from their gardens. (Where *did* she get the idea that British people do this?)

While they were away watching the wonders of wildebeest migration she felt bleak and disappointed. After such a big build-up it was hard to accept that nothing was to come of it. However, she was reassured and comforted by God's presence and a strong feeling that he was telling her he had someone for her, and she must just be patient.

A week later they were back in Nairobi again, and unusually, so was Colin. They went to hear him preach on the Sunday, and afterwards went with a group of people to the cinema to see *Shrek 2*. Roni paid careful attention to the places where he laughed and noted that he found the funny bits funny. She had also found his sermon inspiring and thought-provoking. She began to feel less resolved about her conclusions of the week before. Maybe God had a different list from hers, and maybe the places where Colin didn't match her requirements weren't important? That night she prayed, 'Please God, if this is the man for me, please could he offer to take me out for lunch and to the airport tomorrow.' Fifteen minutes later, the offer came to take her out for lunch and to the airport.

Colin really pulled out the stops to impress her the next day, taking her for a slap-up meal of intestines in a road-side kiosk. She was relieved to discover he spoke fluent Swahili, as this indicated he was unlikely to be heading for the suburban English garden-vacuuming scenario that she so despised. By the time the last scrap of intestine had gone from their plates Col was trying to recruit her to work at A Rocha, Kenya. (Nice turn-around Col! Not so much of the 'volunteer outfit' talk now he'd discovered manly Ronnie was gorgeous girlie Roni.)

A hefty correspondence ensued and they began to get to know each other over email and through texting. During this time, Roni struggled with God over the ways in which Col was different to the man she had been so diligently designing in her mind over the preceding years. The crunch came one night when she heard the clearest communication from God that she had ever experienced. And he said, referring to Colin, 'Here is the man I have chosen for you to marry.' She took this revelation to her pastor, and to some friends, who all confirmed they felt it was from God. So, with a strange mixture of sadness and pain from the demise of her dream man, and peace and excitement about what was to transpire with Col, she got on a plane and went to spend some time with him in Kenya. Within the first five days of being together, any doubts had dissipated, and she felt sure at last that she had found 'The One'.

The engagement followed very shortly after this – in a matter of days. They were searching for a rare bird in remote woodland, and under the moonlight with the elusive Sokoke Scops owl hooting sadly and the moonlight casting haunting shadows through the trees Col dropped down on one knee and proposed. Roni answered without the slightest hesitation, 'Of course I will!'

The next day they chose a ring: a red ruby (What else?) from Kenya, with a small Namibian diamond on either side, set in South African gold. Then Col phoned Roni's dad to negotiate the number of cattle he needed to pay for her hand in marriage, and they were set!

Seeking the Will of God

It is right and good to want to follow God's will in the major decisions in your life, and the choice of who to marry certainly qualifies. The question is, does he always have a specific person in mind for you? And if he does, how do you find out who it is? Here are my conclusions to these questions – feel free to disagree with me. I know some of you will.

I tend to think that the first and most important way to know God's will, his opinion on things, is to know God. This means knowing his word through scripture (although not necessarily blindly imitating any scenario you find enacted therein – see below), knowing his presence through the Holy Spirit, in prayer and worship, becoming more like him as you live in daily obedience to him, and living in community with his followers who will also reflect something of who he is. If you are investing in a life lived closely with God, you are more likely to want the things he does, for the reasons he does, and you don't need to contort yourself with anxiety and frustration looking for extra signs and wonders to confirm everything you want to do.

Sometimes, God will make it uncontrovertibly obvious how he'd like things to work out. He certainly pulled out the stops for Col and Roni. Their story involves visions, strange 'coincidences', just about audible divine speech, uniquely designed jewellery, confirmation from scripture and Christian friends, and major doses of inner peace at the necessary junctures. Roni points out that, in their case, without this help along the way there would have been very little likelihood of them ever crossing paths, and even if they had they wouldn't have had a chance to get to know each other well enough for a decision like marriage. Also, she needed huge encouragement from God to be able to face the changes that marrying Colin brought about. In one plane journey she changed countries, friends, language, job and marital status. It was a major upheaval, and one she might not have been able to countenance without plentiful signs and wonders confirming it was the right thing to do.

God acts differently in different situations and with different people. This is because he is God and can do that. We can't get bossy and demanding and insist he act in the same way with us, just to be fair. Mostly, we are given a lot of discretion to make our own choices based on general truths and principles, together with our desires and common sense. These general truths would include the fact that God has made it clear we should marry one person, of the opposite sex, who is not already married to someone else and who is also a follower of God. Our desires tell us if we want to marry the person or not. Our common sense will hopefully help us discern if we are compatible and likely to enjoy life together or whether there is a chance we are going to rip each other apart with frustration. If you find you are hanging back from committing to marriage with a person, waiting for a voice to boom from the clouds telling you what to do, maybe, just maybe, your hesitation has more to do with the fact you don't really want to marry that person, but you are reluctant to take responsibility for your decision.

As to whether God has someone specific in mind for who you marry... well, this is a tricky one. There are definitely couples who seem to be brought together according to divine purpose. There are many more who hang on to this idea as a way of making it through difficult patches when without that consolation they might well have gone their separate ways. And then there are those who in godly faithfulness weighed up the options and made the best decision they could. Once married, that is the person for you and the person you have become one with. Could there have been others you might have married and been happy with? At the risk of engendering some opposition here, I would want to say yes, I believe so. If you have experienced many instances of unmistakable guidance as you approached your own decision, I am happy for you, and glad that God has blessed you in this way. If not, don't sweat it. Stay close to God and trust your instincts, and he will have his hand on your marriage also.

How Does It Happen in the Bible?

There are some who look to the Bible for guidance on everything. 'Not a bad thing to do', you might say. But it does depend on how you see it guiding you. It would not be wise to follow the example of the weird and wonderful cast of characters found within its pages. As one of my Regent professors used to say, 'God is the only hero in this book.' Here is a list of ways that Biblical characters went about choosing a spouse. (I stole this from someone who stole it from someone else... thank you to whoever had the original idea. I am indebted.)

1. Get God to make you someone while you lie snoring in bed. When you wake up, there they'll be.

   ...the Lord God caused the man to fall into a deep sleep... then the Lord God made a woman from the rib he had taken out of the man, and he brought her to the man. (Genesis 2: 21, 22)

2. Find a man with seven daughters (or sons) and do your best to impress him.

Now a priest of Midian had seven daughters and they came to draw water and fill the troughs to water their father's flock. Some shepherds came along and drove them away, but Moses got up and came to their rescue... When the girls returned to Reuel their father, he asked them, 'Why have you returned so early today?' They answered, 'An Egyptian rescued us from the shepherds...' 'And where is he?' he asked his daughters. 'Why did you leave him? Invite him to have something to eat.' Moses agreed to stay with the man, who gave his daughter Zipporah to Moses in marriage. (Exodus 2: 16–21)

3. Marry a captive.

If you notice among the captives a beautiful woman and you are attracted to her, you may take her as your wife. Bring her into your house and have her shave her head, trim her nails and put aside the clothes she was wearing when captured. After she has lived in your house and mourned for her father and mother for a full month, then you may go to her and be her husband and she shall be your wife. (Deuteronomy 21: 11–13)

4. When you see someone you like, let your parents know and get them to sort it out for you.

I have seen a Philistine woman in Timnah; now get her for me.
If they question you, simply respond by saying,

Get her for me. She's the right one for me. (Judges 14: 2–3)

5. Go to a party and hide. When the women come out to dance, grab one and carry her off.

Go and hide in the vineyards and watch. When the young women of Shiloh come out to join in the dancing, then rush from the vineyards and each of you seize a wife. (Judges 21: 20–21)

6. Purchase a piece of property that has a wife or husband included in the price.

On the day you buy the land from Naomi, you also acquire Ruth the Moabite, the dead man's widow, in order to maintain the name of the dead with his property. (Ruth 4: 5)

7. Lower your standards and make up for quality with quantity.

King Solomon… loved many foreign women… He had seven hundred wives of royal birth and three hundred concubines. (1 Kings 11: 1–3)

8. Become the leader of a huge nation and hold a contest. Marry the winner.

Let a search be made for beautiful young virgins for the king… and let beauty treatments be given to them. Then let the young woman who pleases the king be queen… (Esther 2: 2–4)

Spiritual Manipulation

It is conceivable that God may somehow communicate to you the person you should marry before that person is aware of it. If this should happen, may I strongly advise that you ponder it in your heart, as Mary did with the news of her unexpected pregnancy, and wait to see how things unfold? Going to the person and telling them to fall in line with the divine information you have been privileged to receive will have several possible outcomes, none of which is particularly desirable:

a) They will think you are a fruit loop, laugh in your face and tell anecdotes about you at future dinner parties. ('Once this guy told me God said I had to marry him – no kidding! Ha ha ha'.)

b) They will have secretly been in love with you, but will be crushed that you are only after them because God told you to be and not because you love them back, and they will be hurt and sad and confused.

c) They will be battered into submission by your holy rhetoric and agree to marry you but without really wanting to. They may start to really dislike God (not to mention how they will feel about you, his mouthpiece).

So, instead, test what you think you have heard from God by praying, getting to know the person and seeing where things go. Once they have received communication from the Lord along the same lines, or at the very least peace and certainty about the relationship, and only then, should the contentious cat be let out of the bag. Any earlier and it might scratch someone's eyes out.

Questions

If you are someone who needs supernatural confirmation for all your decisions, getting engaged is going to be no exception. God in his gracious kindness might well help you out here – he seems to work with us very individually according to how we best communicate with him. I hope these questions will help you as you try to discern what to do:

1. Are you generally close to God at the moment? Are things right between you? Are you nourishing your spiritual life with the Bible, time spent in prayer and in worship with others?
2. Do you love, respect and like the person you are thinking about marrying? Are they a committed Christian too? Do you have common goals in life? Do you share a sense of humour? Do you find them attractive?
3. Have you tested any signs, prophecies or inner promptings by checking them out against the Bible, with other Christians and with your common sense?
4. Have you got a history of hearing from God and acting in obedience? Do you trust your instincts in this?

5

Love in the Twilight Years

y grandmother was widowed when she was barely seventy, which these days makes her relatively young. She and Grandpa were very happy together, but she was not someone to relish living alone, and after about a year, she and I started having chats about boys. When I teased her about finding a nice gentleman to gad about town with, she would become coy and girly, and even seemed to encourage the conversation rather than shutting it down as I expected her to. In the event, she died not long after Grandpa, and as far as I know, still hadn't gone on any dates, but she had got me thinking. People do live for longer now, and why should they not seek intimate companionship in the latter years? Old age can be lonely, and younger generations of family are no longer guaranteed to live in the same country let alone the same town. Even if they are local, life has become busier and work commitments more entangling. Family members are not often able to provide the care and company that we need at any stage of life, but never more so than during the final stretch. Plus, retirement can bring ample social opportunities to scout out the talent – think bingo, ballroom dancing, bus tours round stately homes and gardens, golfing and croquet –

as well as the time to devote to gentle flirtation and intrigue. And if true love should burst upon this sedate scene, all the better.

Peter and Kay

I interviewed Peter and Kay just two weeks after their wedding, and the glow of the day was still visible on their faces. Well, not just the glow of the day, but the glow of amazement that they have found each other. This romance has sneaked in during the later stages of full lives lived well... Peter is eighty, and Kay, a young sixty.

The previous time I had seen Peter, who is my brother-in-law's grandfather, was not long after his second wife had died. He looked sad and tired, and at least as old as his years. Heather had been suffering from dementia for the previous five years and he had been daily challenged by her smouldering cigarettes left in the bedclothes, the trips down the village high street in her lacy nightwear and her single-minded and devious attempts to get behind the wheel and go for a drive. The health visitor advised him to get an immobilizer, but he didn't want to demean her or treat her like a child. He was to the end, as Kay put it, 'loyal and steadfast'.

The contrast between those distressing times, and this particular October Saturday that I had come to talk to the newly-weds, was like the 'before and after' on an extreme makeover show. It was not that he looked plastic or surgically altered, but just that the difference was too profound to be explained by superficialities of style and presentation (although I have to say the pink shirt was undeniably good with his colouring). The man who greeted me at the door was younger, happier and more sparkly than I had ever seen him. His dog, incidentally, who also greeted me at the door, is a very strange shape and looks more like a Picasso painting of a dog than a real-life dog. Sorry dog – I did like you, but you are quite lumpy. Not that you can help that, you poor thing. Or your wind problem.

Back to the human protagonists. The woman single-handedly responsible for Peter's transformation is Kay, headteacher of the village primary school. She and Peter had known each other socially and by reputation (an outstandingly good reputation I should add – and I have that from outside sources) for over twenty years before any rumblings of romance stirred between them. They both sat on the same committees, had a common interest in the cricket club, the drama society and pretty much everything else going in the village. By the time Peter was widowed, Kay had been alone for eleven years. Following her divorce, she had sole care and responsibility for her daughter who has learning difficulties and she felt this was a complication that would hinder any future relationship. She had become reconciled to her independence and self-sufficiency, and surrounded by friends, was not lonely.

Six months after Heather's death, Peter was taken by his daughter to The George for lunch. Spotting Kay in a corner with a friend, he walked over and gave her a hug. It crossed his mind that if he had been twenty years younger... but at seventy-nine it just wouldn't be fair on the delightful lady he had momentarily in his arms. Her friend hugged him too, and they told him he was one of their favourite men.

At a birthday party for a mutual friend a couple of months later, Kay came over to tell him she would be away for the next ten days. While she was gone, Peter missed her and determined to call her when she got back. Whether you are eighty or eight, calling a girl you like is a daunting task: he was extremely relieved when she didn't pick up the phone, as he had no clue what he was going to say. But he was not about to be deterred – all that was needed was a different approach. Gathering his courage, he went down to the school in person, and requested a meeting with Kay to discuss Clare, a girl who had been cleaning for him part-time and also cleaned at the school. After covering this rather random agenda, he said a formal 'Thank you' and leaving a bemused Kay looking after him, walked home wondering how on earth to engineer another meeting. Realizing that this under-hand, indirect approach was going to be very time con-suming, he did the honourable and straightforward thing (hint: we girls like this way of doing things) and asked her out for lunch. In honour of the occasion he bought a new linen sports jacket – the fact he told me this detail is just one of the reasons I like him so much. On the drive to the Roman villa that he had chosen as the location of this momentous date, he says he drove 'carefully'. Kay told me that the word 'carefully' does not quite capture the caution of that journey: apparently, he didn't get out of third gear for the entire thirty-three miles! Not a boy racer then. Do older men drive as slowly as possible to impress their dates, while younger men go fast, I wonder?

By the end of the day, they had recognized a depth of character in each other that is only formed through suf-fering. They found a whole range of commonalities and discovered an ease in each other's company that they had not found with anyone else. And Peter would want me to mention that he found her looks entrancing and delightful – he is still trying to convince her of the objective truth of her beauty. I hope he manages, because she really is lovely and it would be a shame for her to be ignorant of this fact for much longer.

Very shortly after this promising first date, Peter began to start sentences with the rather presumptuous phrase, 'When we're married...' to which Kay would respond, 'Hurry slowly', anxious not to rush things along too fast. The fateful lunch at the Roman villa had been in July; in December, Peter had an eightieth birthday party, celebrated by just forty close family members (just forty you cry! I know – I was impressed too), and Kay. The whole clan proceeded to fall in love with her en masse, and she with them.

The Thursday before Christmas they went into Salisbury for some late-night shopping, and outside Carter's jewellery shop, Peter said pragmatically, 'Well, we might as well get a ring.' This was a man on a mission if you ask me. Her defences must have been worn down because she made no resistance to the ring suggestion, and there was no more talk of hurrying slowly.

With three previous marriages and 140 years of life between them Peter and Kay still felt that to make public vows and officially belong together was the natural outcome of the love they had for one another; as Peter put it, it 'wraps it all up'. They had found with each other deep companionship and understanding, and to commit to each other for the rest of their lives made perfect sense.

As we finished up our tea and I prepared to take my leave, I asked this evidently contented couple what advice they would give to younger people facing the life changing decision of whether to get married and if so, to whom. These were their words of wisdom:

1. You have to want to share your life and give to the other person.
2. You have to think about the logistics of finances, circumstance, timing, etc., and as there will always be obstacles, ask yourself whether you love the person enough to overcome them.
3. You need to be content and secure in who you are, and be willing to be vulnerable.

Deciding to Marry in Later Life

In many ways, the process of committing to someone for the rest of your life is the same however many years you anticipate the rest amounting to (Peter and Kay have a pact with each other that they will have at least fifteen years together: I'll drink to that). But there is some wisdom that comes from having lived for longer that can be of great benefit. I am sure that Peter and Kay have no illusions about marriage being the answer to all their social, emotional, physical and spiritual needs. For younger people entering marriage, these illusions are a potential hazard, and put a great burden on the early years as cherished ideals get painfully chipped into a more realistic shape. Wiser and older people know that no one is perfect and that adjustments will have to be made. They also know that change is possible, positive and is destined to continue until your last breath. Change is a far more daunting prospect if you have not yet lived through much.

Self-knowledge is not always the result of living with yourself over a long period of time, but it can be, and if it is, then it will certainly help you as you choose whether or not to marry someone. Knowing yourself means you will know the sort of person you usually get along well with, the kinds of things that rub you up the wrong way, how you communicate and what makes you happy. Insights like these will be useful to you in the romantic arena.

It is quite probable that if you are considering marriage in the latter stages of life you will have had plenty of experience of being unmarried, whether you have been single to this point, or whether you have been divorced or widowed. You know what it is to be alone and you won't take the other person for granted. Unless, of course, you have relished living alone, and developed all sorts of unsociable habits, such as drinking orange juice straight from the carton, going to sleep with the light on and allowing the cat to sleep on your pillow. Independence can be appealing and hard to relinquish, but there are two things to say about that. Firstly, a good marriage will still give you plenty of breathing space. Kay and Peter specifically mentioned how they each appreciated the way the other had plenty of interests and friendships that they pursued individually, and how that enriched the time they had together. Marriage is not, and should not be, the end of self-hood. Secondly, independence can be a euphemism for selfishness, and it is a good thing for selfishness to be challenged.

Previous marriages could help or hinder the process of getting engaged as a pensioner. An experience of a long and happy marriage will mean you know that marriage is essentially a good thing, and so will predispose you to find that sort of commitment a positive move. Conversely, you could fear that no one else will live up to your late husband or wife. An unhappy marriage could have left long-term scars, leaving a person vulnerable and afraid of emotional closeness. But the flip side of that is that you might be more eager to redeem your past and pursue a better relationship.

Till Death Do Us Part

No marriage is free from the spectre of death. A friend of mine has just got engaged in the shadow of a cancer diagnosis – they are particularly aware of the precious fragility of their time together. We all should have this awareness: there is no knowing what is around the corner, but often we choose to live as though we are immune to loss. When a couple get married at an advanced age, there is no getting away from the fact that there is simply less sand in the egg timer. There will be days when it all slips away far too fast, but on good days, the sand will turn to gold dust, every grain full of value and so beautiful.

There is also the need to face the reality that old age often brings with it illness, disability and general physical and mental deterioration. It is easy to understand holding people back from wanting to marry at this stage – there would be the fear of having to sustain and care for a needy human being, as well as the risk of having to be the needy human yourself. Most of us entering marriage do so with the firm intention of withstanding the storms of hardship, but hoping our intentions won't be too strongly tested. For some the hardship is immediate and consuming.

Tidings of Great Joy

For some people, the final years of life are a gradual decline – a time of tartan slippers, false teeth, a closer relationship with your GP than you ever really wanted, snooker on the telly and a rigid timetable of tea consumption. (If this is starting to sound comfortable and appealing and you are still in your twenties, may I make a gentle suggestion: GET A LIFE!) To become engaged and then married at this point has the same effect as jump-starting a failing car battery and discovering the old banger has many more miles of road it can cover before it needs to splutter up to the junk yard and park for good. There is suddenly so much to live for, so much hope and love and romance to be squeezed into the final chapter. How wonderful to live out your days *really living*, and counting each day as a blessing not a burden? I still marvel at the memory of Peter opening the front door such a rejuvenated and joyful incarnation of himself, and would wish similar happiness on all senior citizens everywhere.

Questions

At this stage of life, I anticipate that you know your own mind. So just a few red lights to look out for. In the manner of a glossy magazine quiz, if you have answered yes to more than one of these questions, seriously consider pulling out!

1. Are you very rich and is your fiancé very young?
2. Do you ever forget their name? Do you ever forget yours?
3. Do you get angry if the BBC reschedules your soap to report on a world disaster?
4. Do you prefer the company of animals to people?
5. Do these questions make you extremely uncomfortable?

6

Childhood Sweethearts

While working as an au pair in Muswell Hill, I would sometimes look after the little boy from down the road as well as my own charges. He was the same age as Isobel, my two-year-old charge, and whenever I pushed them in the double buggy together they would hold hands. Sitting in front of *Sesame Street* they would cuddle up on the bean bag like teens in the back of the cinema and they would even share their apple chunks and carrot sticks. It seemed as though they had found true love as toddlers.

Wouldn't it be great if life were that simple? I'm sure Joshua and Isobel both found new distractions in the playground, and will probably pass in and out of numerous relationships of varying gravity before finding a marriage partner. Isobel was showing signs of becoming a proficient flirt before mastering basic language skills so I am especially sure she has an interesting romantic future ahead of her. But imagine for a second that they were each other's one and only love interest. Do you envy or pity them their lifelong devotion? As someone who designed my wedding dress when I was still drawing arms coming out of heads, the thought appeals to me somewhat. You would never have the awful moments of feeling convinced that there was no one in the world for you, and you would have the security of knowing you were the centre of someone's universe throughout the dreadful self-doubt of the teenage years. Plus, you could keep your friends loyal by threatening not to let them be a bridesmaid if they stepped out of line.

But I paint a rather sentimental picture here – let's face it, who *really* ever marries someone they played footsie with in their highchairs? And isn't there something good and healthy about dabbling a bit with the world of romance before entering the solemn realm of matrimony?

Before we go into the complexities and pros and cons of prolific dating and meeting at this life stage or that, I want to introduce you to my friends Bekah and Joel who became a couple as teenagers. This, although rare, is a more likely scenario than the pre-potty-trained pair of Muswell Hill I mentioned earlier, and might well be a situation similar to the one you find yourself in.

Bekah and Joel

Last weekend, Shawn and I went to the wedding of the last of my university housemates to get married. At the reception we sat at a table of four couples who knew each other from those days, with three children and one on the way between us. Despite the eagerness with which we attempted to get to the front of the queue for the creperie that was the glorious culmination of the meal, we appeared to have entered a new phase of life.

Bekah and Joel, who make up one of these disconcertingly grown-up couples, have known each other through many of the life phases passed through so far.

Their relationship began when Bekah was seventeen and Joel sixteen, and apart from one unhappy night in a Lake District youth hostel, they have been a couple ever since. They were one of the certainties at university – whatever else changed in the world, whatever misguided relationships the rest of us passed in and out of, Bekah and Joel would be together.

They met at a church youth group, which in Bekah's recollection was a seething stew of sordid intrigue. If one turned away while two people were cuddling, on turning back two seconds later they would each be cuddling someone else. Nearly all possible dating combinations were attempted in an ever changing kaleidoscope of pairings. Joel and Bekah were immersed in this unwholesome behaviour for a short while, but their relationship saved them from most of it.

Joel remembers meeting Bekah when he approached her after she'd been singing up front, to thank her for her worship leading. While he had an honest appreciation of her vocal ability, perhaps what compelled him more persuasively to make the approach was his even stronger appreciation of her posterior! She doesn't remember their first meeting, Joel's behind evidently making less of an impression than her own, but she vividly recalls a weekend they went on, supposedly organized to help them revise for exams: I can't imagine much revision going on with that particular youth group though, unless it was revising who you had a crush on. She was sitting by the football field where Joel was playing (super-athletically I'm sure, with such inspiration on the sideline) gazing dejectedly at the hills in the distance and feeling miserable about a guy she was horribly and hopelessly infatuated with at the time. Joel saw his

opportunity, and, coming to sit beside her, delivered a
line that soothed her aching heart instantly: 'Those hills
look beautiful. Would you like to go for a walk there?'
Well, put like that, yes of course she did! They had their
first kiss the next day, but then decided they ought to get
to know each other before being in a relationship. So
they waited for three days and then Joel phoned her and
asked her out.

For the next two years Bekah expected Joel to break
up with her at any moment. He describes her during that
time as an 'emotional heap'. She suffered from chronic
low self-esteem and found Joel's obvious devotion hard
to accept at face value. From his perspective, he was well
and truly in love by six months in and had no intention
of letting her get away. While still in the early days of
their relationship, he played her U2's song 'I Still Haven't
Found What I'm Looking For' and then gave her a card
in which he'd written, 'I've found what I'm looking for.'

Joel comes from a wonderful, if slightly conservative,
missionary family. His parents had laid down the rule
that he was not to date until he was eighteen, so there was
some initial resistance to his relationship with Bekah.
The first time he brought her home to meet them he pre-
ceded the ordeal by winding Bekah up and issuing dire
warnings about their disapproval and dislike of her and
had her understandably flustered and terrified. Despite
the hot day she wore a long-sleeved shirt buttoned up to
her neck so as not to offend them, and sat nervously sip-
ping lemonade on the edge of her seat trying to make
proper small talk. It was not long before she realized Joel
had perhaps been exaggerating some of the drama of the
situation, and she soon became a part of the family. Joel
had a slightly harder time with Bekah's family – one of

her brothers once slammed the front door in his face when he arrived at her house hot and thirsty after a seven-mile cycle. However, over time they became more welcoming and he was usually granted entry to the house!

When Bekah left school she worked for a year and then went to America for five weeks, where she went on what she calls a 'doubt spree' inspired by a Bible study she did, looking at the story of Abraham being asked by God to sacrifice his son Isaac. The notes she was using urged the reader to be willing to sacrifice anything of worth and value in their lives. She started to worry that she ought to give up Joel, and when she came back from America, she announced that she needed to be 'just friends' until she could get her head sorted out. Several weeks later, Joel remarked casually that if they were going on holiday together to visit family as planned, they needed to book their air tickets that week. Amazingly, he had forgotten what she had said about just being friends, which explained why he had seemed so laid back about the whole thing. They went on the holiday, and things continued on as before.

While they had clicked from their first conversation and talked in terms of 'forever' in the way that teenagers in love do, they both wondered if things would change once they started university. Bekah had the realization that there were other potential boyfriends out there, and Joel struggled with knowing his dreams of rugged and carefree travel post-graduation might have to be sacrificed. Neither of these issues were enough to make them seriously consider breaking up though, and their commitment became perhaps even more secure, made with full awareness that it was a choice, and there were other choices that could be made but weren't.

Bekah began to battle with bad health during her second year at university. She was eventually diagnosed with fibromyalgia, but for months endured mysterious and debilitating symptoms of fatigue, painful joints and insomnia. Joel took on a caring role and the dynamics of their relationship changed drastically for a time. Having to work through something so serious and difficult together brought them a new understanding of love as it plays out for better and for worse. At the same time, friends of theirs at the same age and stage overtook them on the inside lane and got engaged after a speedy romance, making Bekah feel that if others had got engaged, she and Joel who had been together far longer, ought to be engaged too. It was deeply aggravating to be pipped to the post. Joel, while reassuring her that he had every intention of marrying her, also felt strongly that they ought to finish their studies before becoming Mr and Mrs, and didn't want a long engagement. Unjust though it seemed, the dating phase was set to continue a while longer.

Twelve long months later they were both ready for the next step, and went to speak to Bekah's parents. In many cases this is just a formality – it is rare in this day and age either for parents to express strong views on their off-spring's decisions or for offspring to pay any attention to the strong views even if they are expressed. In this par-ticular situation, both a-typical scenarios were played out. Bekah's mother and father felt that they should be established in the working world before marrying, to avoid the financial stresses that they had themselves experienced getting married part way through a PhD. While Bekah and Joel did not have the same anxieties about financial stability, and had no intention of waiting a few more years before marrying, they wanted to respect the desire for caution and patience that lay behind the advice and so put their plans to become formally engaged on hold. As a housemate watching in the wings, I can attest to how painful and costly this decision was for them, and only have admiration for the way they handled it.

The progression of their relationship was not to be halted indefinitely by this set back, however, and the day came when they were to get engaged. Bekah had guessed when it was to happen, and our whole household was fizzing with excitement when Joel came to pick her up. They had chosen a ring some time before, and Bekah had bought him an electric screwdriver to commemorate the event (a kind and thoughtful gift, the memory of which makes her cringe!), and with these important items stashed carefully away in the car, they set off to the hills where they had gone on that historic first walk together. There was much squealing and cooing and general unbridled girliness on their return to our house, and all of us, but most especially the affianced couple, felt a profound sense of relief that they could now get on with the business of planning a wedding and a life together.

A month before Bekah and Joel first met, Bekah's religious studies teacher had her class write down a list of the qualities their ideal man would possess. Her list included the following: dark hair, musical, cultured, romantic and caring. The one non-negotiable was that he be musical. At first glance Joel bears absolutely no resemblance to the man she was describing. One of her main hang-ups about their relationship in the early days was that she was musical and he was sporty, and how could they possibly be compatible? Despite this glaring chasm of difference between them, they are one of the most well-suited couples you could hope to meet. Perhaps they have grown to be alike as they have known each other through such formative years. However it has happened, they have an amazingly strong friendship, an obvious enjoyment of each other's company, respect for each other's minds and even after all these years flirt with each other outrageously in public.

Travelling Hand Luggage

My philosophy on relationships post-puberty was that it was far better to be in one than not if you could arrange it. Most of the time I couldn't – I wasn't on the list of girls approved for dating purposes at my school, so I tried to cram in plenty of holiday romances and mooned excessively over unobtainable and unsuitable boys at school during term time. By the end of university, I had quite a trail of emotional debris in my wake, and decided a two-year period of total dating abstinence was probably the best move. I met my husband Shawn at the end of this time. Now when I talk to the girls in my youth group, and they tell me that all they want for Christmas is a boyfriend, I sympathize painfully, but I find myself saying: 'Girls, it's all baggage. Try and hold off. Boys are not the only important thing in life.' What a hypocrite I am! But I really do wish I had done things differently. Each relationship you have that doesn't end in marriage ends in a break up, inevitably causing both parties a degree of distress. A little bit of you will be chipped off, and your heart will be that much tougher. You will have intimate memories of sharing emotions and experiences with someone who is not your husband or wife. Because of their influence in shaping who you become, they will be a shadowy presence that accompanies you through the years. In short, they will be awkward, cumbersome luggage. So there is one advantage of meeting your spouse early on in life: no troublesome exes to contend with.

Having indulged in a tirade of one-sided fanaticism about dating as little as possible before getting married, I feel compelled to cool down and temper my passionate words with a cautious peek at another perspective, which I am sure you are hopping up and down trying to get across to me through the page. Can't hear you, sorry! But maybe you are saying something like this: 'Excuse me, some of us have very happy memories of the boyfriends/girlfriends we had as teens and in our twenties. We learnt a lot about ourselves and about relating to other people and this helped us know what sort of person we wanted to marry. And we are glad to be the people we are now – because that is who our fiancés love, and we don't mind that we were influenced by previous relationships. In this day and age, you can't expect to meet someone with a pristine history, and if you did you might wonder if there was something wrong with them. Would no one date them and if not, why not? Do they have normal human emotions? And before you shut us up and start writing from your own perspective again, we'd like to say that at least we will never wonder if we are missing out when we settle down with one person for the rest of our lives – from our previous experiences we will be more aware of the other options out there. And, and...' Right, enough from you – this is my book.

Somewhere in the middle of these two sides lies the elusive happy medium. I have to agree that we always learn from relationships we have been in, and often we learn positive lessons about our own worth, how to treat another human being and how to balance an intense relationship with the rest of life which continues to need our attention. At the same time, it is a good idea to maintain standards and be a bit selective about who we become romantically involved with, bearing in mind they will contribute to shaping who we become, and may teach us unfortunate lessons – that people are not to be trusted or that we don't deserve to be adored and cared for. Someone once told me, in the portentous tones that tend to stick in one's mind for decades, that anyone I dated and who I didn't end up marrying was likely to end up as someone else's husband or wife, and should therefore be treated how I'd want someone to treat my future spouse if they were dating them at the time. That kind of puts things in perspective. On the other hand, you can't assume that just because you were still a moody adolescent when you met that you won't get married to each other. Bekah's advice to you if you find yourself in a serious relationship at a young age is to keep an open mind; don't rush ahead and plan your future together too early, but likewise don't assume that it won't work out just because you are young.

Life has its choices and with each choice comes an abandonment of the choice you didn't make – you take one road, and this means you never go down all those enticing other roads. If you marry your childhood sweetheart, you are likely to have to make certain sacrifices and perhaps turn your back on dreams you might have had for how your life would turn out. It is vital that you reconcile yourself to this early on, and don't become bitter towards the other person for standing in the way of your travelling rock star lifestyle, or the silence of the conventrefectory you imagined yourself eating in three times a day.

Flying Long Haul

Meeting the love of your life early on means that in all probability you will have a relatively long dating relationship. Our culture tends to frown on those who marry 'too young' and casts doubts on the likelihood of marital success in the case of unwrinkled brides and smooth-chinned grooms. Many choose to complete their education, see the world, and at least start ascending the wearisome ladder of career success before tying the knot. To cast a positive light on this situation, you will end up marrying someone you know extremely well – someone you will have seen on top of the world and hitting the depths, someone who you will have seen change and grow and mature, someone as familiar to you as yourself. Your shared history will form a strong bond between you, and you will have already proved to yourself and others that you can make the relationship work. On the negative side of things, the fizzle factor of the early days will be a long way behind you, and you will have to make the decision to marry in a far more cerebral fashion, without the temporary madness of love chemicals rushing you blindly over the cliff of lifelong commitment whatever the cost. You will know that romance and fickle feelings are not the only basis for a lasting relationship, but you might have a nagging sense of flatness that makes you wonder if you should cut ties and run off looking for the intoxication with someone else.

If you are Christians and have managed to stay sexually chaste, this will have meant some serious repression and frustration over the years, that those who meet and marry in a flash do not have to deal with. When you eventually do marry and can have all the God-sanctioned nooky you could possibly desire, you may find your strategies for repression have become a bit more embedded than is helpful in the new dispensation.

There are both advantages and disadvantages in marrying your childhood sweetheart and consequently having an extremely long dating relationship. You could perhaps say that the flight was longer so you got stiff and restless, but you got to watch movies and the end destination was worth the air miles.

Passports Please

I started using an air travel metaphor for my subheadings, so to continue in the same vein, passports refer to identity. There is a phase of life known as the 'formative years', when we figure out who we are, take on some influences and reject others, and generally emerge as a more fully-rounded person at the other end. If we meet our life partner during these years, we are going to find that they have had significant input into the form of the final product. Ideally, we will be in a relationship with a person who allows us space to become who we are supposed to be, to develop diverse interests and arrive at views and opinions that may be different from theirs. The danger lies in becoming so intertwined with another person at this stage that we distort each other's shape and inhibit each other's growth into maturity.

Bekah mentioned the fact that because she had not been single since she was sixteen she would not know herself outside of a relationship should anything, forbid the thought, happen to Joel. But that is going to be true for anyone once they have been married for a few years I should think. Other than this tragic possibility, she tends to see their influence on each other as purely advantageous. When they got married they had to make very little adjustment to each other's ways as they had been a part of how they had turned out anyway. For a couple who meet and get married once they are more established in adult lives there is going to be much more friction over habits, values and quirks of character that have developed over the years.

Buying Your Ticket

If you have been boyfriend and girlfriend from time immemorial, it might be that getting engaged is a very easy and natural decision to make. You may have assumed for some time that this was going to happen and just be waiting for the right time. You know you can sustain this relationship, you know just about everything there is to know about this person and that you still love them, and you know you can't contemplate life without them. The element of risk is much lower than for many couples contemplating this step.

However, there could be complications specific to this sort of relationship too. I don't wish to be sexist, but I have the feeling that men in particular might wonder about shutting the door on all those unsampled delights of female companionship out in the big wide world so early. And after all the years of ambling along in a stable relationship the momentum to kick things up a gear might be lacking. But for those who can overcome these obstacles and arrive safely in the land of marriage, the future looks bright.

Questions

If you are contemplating marriage to your childhood sweet-heart, you might want to consider these questions:

1. How does the thought of life without this person make me feel?
2. In what ways has this relationship enabled me to grow, mature and become the person I want to be? How have I enabled my partner to grow?
3. Has this relationship mostly made me happy? Has it been a positive part of my life so far?
4. Am I still here out of choice or habit?
5. What sacrifices will I have to make to commit to this person for life? Does any part of me resent these? Have I made my peace with them?
6. What input have I had about relationships and how they work? What good and bad examples have I observed? What books have I read? Who have I talked to about issues concerning marriage?

7

A Match Made in Cyber Space

Once upon a time, a woman looked at her diary and realized that now would be a good time to meet a husband. So she paid membership fees to an internet dating site, uploaded a decent photo of herself on a beach (but not in a bikini – she was after a classy catch and didn't want the wrong sort of response) and wrote what she hoped was an intriguing paragraph detailing her key attributes. Once this was accomplished, all she had to do was wait, and she did not have to wait long. Men came from far and wide seeking to correspond with her, and she held court by her laptop considering their merits. And lo, soon she was in regular typed communication with a handful of the most hopeful prospects, until one day the time was ripe to make telephone contact with her favourite of them all. In the fullness of time, they met and in person he was not the disappointment he might have been. Rings were exchanged and eventually vows, and they thanked their lucky stars that they had found each other. Together against the odds, they lived happily ever after.

It is possible to do all sorts of useful things on the Internet – we can look up the weather forecast in Dubai (hot), Google ourselves, air our opinions on the bizarre behaviour of celebrities and find out what other people think about it, shop for groceries, sell our junk... and find a spouse. I know more and more people who have successfully found their future partner online, and so I think it is fitting to include a pair of cyber love doves in the collection.

Laura and Isuru

Laura is an occupational therapist who I met through work, as she was just embarking on her Internet adventures. When she dropped by our unit she would give us updates on the latest encounter, and we would stop work a while to indulge in some consideration of the diversity of the male species, as illustrated by those who responded favourably to Laura's online profile. It was not looking promising, so imagine our surprise when Mr-Perfectly-Right-For-Laura showed up in her inbox, just as she was on the verge of filing the whole enterprise under the heading of 'Oh Well – Can't Say I Didn't Give it a Good Go'.

As a teenager, Laura had a fairly definite idea in her mind about how her life would unfold. She assumed she would meet her future husband at the age of twenty one, through scouting, and then marry him when she was twenty-six. The scouting thing seemed random to me until she explained that her parents met in this way, as did her sister and her husband. Scouting proved fallow ground for Laura however, and she found her plan had been derailed.

Despite this setback, I don't think she would have turned to the Internet for help had she not been coerced into the speed-dating tent at 'Greenbelt', a Christian arts festival, by friends who wanted to go en-masse. As far as I can gather, speed-dating involves assessing a large number of single members of the opposite sex (in this case) by spending a couple of minutes with each of them, and then ticking a box to say whether you are interested in them or not. If you tick someone who has also ticked you, the organizers facilitate a meeting. Laura didn't tick any boxes, so had no meetings, but she was given a two-week free trial with a Christian online dating agency and that is how it all began. She did not strike lucky at once, but on the way she did gather some good material for amusing anecdotes. A steady stream of unsuitable suitors trooped through her weekends for the following few months.

First in the parade came 'Mr Texter'. After a dull and unpromising evening in a restaurant in Marlow she was taken aback to receive a text on her way home, swiftly followed by another one five minutes after walking through the door, two more before she went to bed, and three during work hours the next day. His seventh text provoked her first reply – short, harsh and to the point: 'I don't like U. I don't want 2 hear from U again.' Fortunately, this message was received loud and clear and Mr Texter absented himself abruptly from her life.

Next up was 'Mr Lawnmower Man', who specialized in fixing broken lawnmowers, as implied by his name. Laura was becoming wise to the game by now and they spent several weeks writing and chatting on the phone before a face-to-face meeting. He even called her nightly on his mobile while on holiday in Portugal. This sweet, blossoming romance was nipped curtly in the bud when they finally did get together. Laura was apparently 'not athletic enough' for Mr Lawnmower.

The crowning glory of these experiences was 'Mr Cinema', a policeman from Windsor. Their first date was, you guessed it, a trip to the cinema. Half way through the movie, he asked her huskily if he could kiss her. She said a prompt and not in the slightest bit husky 'No' at which point he went off to use the toilet and didn't come back.

Meanwhile, out in the Ethernet, a much more hopeful prospect was doing his own searching. Isuru is originally from Southern Asia, but from the age of twenty-three worked in corporate management in more than twenty countries, staying in each for three or four months at a time. His lifestyle was not conducive to a relationship, and by his own admission was centred on money, ambition and power. Family had been of tantamount importance to him as he was growing up, and he realized after four years of putting work before all else that it was important to him now as well, and he would have to make some changes if the possibility of having his own family wasn't to pass him by.

Moving to England, he decided to sign up for an internet dating service. He had very specific ideas about his future wife, and knew that his odds of meeting her coincidentally were very slim. She was to be a fellow Christian, from a strong family, with a good education and an open and caring nature: nothing less would do.

His first response came from a Czech lady. She had three million dollars to get out of the country and needed his bank account number. He responded to her saying, 'You are too rich for me!'

Soon after, he saw Laura's profile on the site, and wrote her a message. Receiving it at work, she read it aloud to her colleagues, who had begun to urge her to give up what they saw as an unhealthy habit, and were disinclined to encourage yet another probable fiasco. She decided this would be her last try, and wrote back a message that Isuru describes as resembling an immigration questionnaire in its depth and scope! Her questions ranged from 'Marmite: yes or no?' to 'I see you put down that you are a Christian – what do you mean by that?' Rather than being put off by this approach, Isuru appreciated the business-like strategy, and felt it got to the core of the issues. He found her questions interesting and sensed she was the sort of person with whom he could carry on a conversation. So their correspondence began in earnest, and by the time they met at Marylebone train station a month later, he had already fallen in love.

Laura had tickets for a concert that evening, and as a way of letting him know how she was feeling the day was progressing, she told him ahead of time that if she didn't invite him to go with her it would mean she wasn't interested in pursuing things. They went for coffee, walked through Green Park, had lunch, and the concert was on.

Talk of marriage followed swiftly. An intense three months later, Isuru made a visit to Laura's dad, respecting the English tradition of asking the bride's father for his blessing. It was given, but not before he had been thoroughly grilled about his visa, his passport and his plans for the future, and specifically, whether he would be taking their beloved daughter to live on the other side of the world.

Meeting their respective families was important to them both. Laura's mum had been tracking the progress of her search, and had trawled through profiles and given her input. She was not at all fazed by the way Isuru had arrived on the scene. Isuru's family believe to this day that they met on a railway station, which I suppose technically they did. Both families gave their whole-hearted support to the relationship before they became officially engaged.

So there was a happy ending to this modern-day fairy story. The engagement ring, by the way, is white gold with a chunky sapphire and six diamonds. Their decision to make this commitment seemed to come relatively easily, and here is my analysis of why that was the case. Both Laura and Isuru approached the dating service with serious intent; they knew they wanted to find a life partner and were looking with that in mind. They had each given thought to the kind of person who they would like to spend their life with, and they quickly recognized the qualities they were hoping for in each other. They were able to corroborate the information they gave each other by meeting friends and family who could confirm the truth of who they were and what they were about. And there was that magic ingredient: chemistry.

I asked them what advice they would give to others on a quest for love in cyber-space. Unsurprisingly, they are inclined to encourage others to take this route, but with a strong cautionary proviso – be careful – have your 'red lights', signals telling you when you should pull out immediately. They both felt that although their meeting was contrived to a degree, that there was still mystery and providence in their coming together. They feel that they should be together, and the fact that a new medium facilitated this doesn't in any way discredit the romance of their story.

Fishing in the Right Pond

How do people meet their future spouses these days? I always thought I would meet my husband at university, where my mum and dad met each other. (Will Laura and Isuru's children assume they will find mates on the Internet I wonder?) You have three years to scope out the talent, and if you do an arts degree like I did, plenty of time for lounging around talking and getting to know people. Somehow, though, out of fifteen thousand or so possible options, I left without having met my Mr Right. I went on dates with a petty criminal called Wolf, a future oil baron from Oman, a hippy and perhaps most unlikely of all, a physics teacher with ultra-conservative views on a woman's role in the church and the home. None of these seemed right somehow. There were just niggling doubts I couldn't get past, or should I say, screamingly obvious flaws in the concept of even a casual relationship with any of these varied and colourful suitors?

My expectations notwithstanding, I don't think university is the most common of places to meet a husband or wife now – apart from anything, we are all getting married much later, and twenty-two seems young to be settling down. So the next best options are church, the pub, the gym, your work place, or one of those organized holidays for singles. A bible college can be good hunting ground, especially if it is one sending its graduates to far-flung outposts once qualified – you might well find a soulmate with plenty in common with you (such as a passion for goat stew) and at the very least there will be plenty of people who don't want to be lonely in the said outpost and are very open to the idea of marriage.

You might just be fortunate enough to have an

incandescent meeting with the love of your life at the supermarket checkout, a friend's wedding or simply in the street, but it is improbable. Having said that, I confess that I once came close to ending up in the script of a romantic 'chick flick'. I was walking up 10th Avenue in West Point Grey, Vancouver, to meet some friends at 'Bean Around the World' (a wittily named coffee shop), when I was stopped by an attractive young man who pointed out that my shoe lace was undone, and offered to do it up for me. I stuck my foot out, he tied my lace, and I went on my way. What a good story that could have been for the grandchildren... except I'm so glad it was such a short episode as Shawn was a few weeks around the corner and will make a much better grandfather. My friend Holly's sister emailed their brother not knowing his email address had changed: let's say the address was johnsmith@hotmail.com. Her brother did not respond, but the new John Smith from Newfoundland who now resided at that address did, and many emails down the line they are married with three small children. I know another girl who met her future spouse on a flight from San Francisco, California to Portland, Oregon, and yet another one who married her surgeon, so these things do happen in real life sometimes.

Right, so let's say you have not met anyone remotely marriageable in all your wanderings through education, workplaces, churches, weddings and leisure facilities, and you really would like to be married. There is nothing wrong with that by the way. Does it not make sense to be more proactive and start shopping around in a more focused manner? Most definitely, if you are brave enough and can forgo the romanticism that would have you trust your love life to the reticent hand of fate, and if you can believe that God can work through modern technology and allows us plenty of leeway to make things happen ourselves.

Here are some sites for you to check out, all specifically targeting Christians. I can't personally vouch for any of them, so please don't sue me if they introduce you to an acrobat from Peru who breaks your heart and runs off with your savings!

- www.christiancafe.com This is based in Canada, and spans Canada, the USA and Europe. It started up in 1998 and claims it has had over a million people try them out since launching.
- www.networkchristians.com Staff at this organization run a matching service by hunting out compatible people on its database. It also organizes day events, meals, weekends, holidays and conferences for singles, which as well as providing a context for meeting potential love interests, encourages people to live the single life well and to the full.
- www.linkchristians.co.uk This site only caters to UK residents. It has around 6,500 members, and users are asked to complete two essay questions to discourage casual browsers.
- www.christianconnection.co.uk This company also has sites for Australia and Germany. It has features including internal email, instant chat and SMS, and it organizes social events for members.

Intentions

Laura and Isuru went down the Internet dating route with the express purpose of finding a spouse. It is worth really searching your heart before you start down this road – do you want to get married? Are you open to the possibility at least that you might find the love of your life this way? By doing this you can hope to avoid hurting those who do have serious intentions, and be able to guard yourself against casual daters more easily.

Having a list of non-negotiable qualities that must be present in a person you would consider marrying isn't a bad idea, as long as it doesn't start looking too much like a shopping list. However comprehensive your list, you will end up with a human being, not a list of attributes, and maybe you don't yet fully know the kind of person you really need or want. I had no idea how great it would be to be married to someone who can fix broken things and understands technology, or how having a big kid for a husband keeps me from indulging my propensity for introspection and intensity, or how important it would be to be married to someone who stays calm and engaged during conflict. I could not, in short, have designed Shawn for myself before I met him. Try to be open to a surprise and don't be too specific in your criteria. Keep away from details such as eye colour, accent, profession, leisure pursuits and choice of newspaper. The non-negotiables are going to vary person to person and you will have to wrestle through these yourself. They might include things such as religious convictions, political convictions, criminal convictions, whether or not they want children, their sense of humour, finding them physically attractive and being able to speak the same language.

Guidelines

There are some inherent risks involved in finding a spouse on the Internet that need to be addressed. In the first instance, it is always possible that the person you think you are getting to know is a fabrication. It is quite easy to make up an identity – name, age, gender, job, location – all can be falsified. Be cautious and careful with your heart until you have had a chance to verify who this person is and whether they are representing themselves truthfully.

Most, if not all, dating sites will offer guidelines for safety. These include ensuring your first meeting is in a public place, making sure someone you trust knows where you are and that you have a means of contacting them, and not getting into the person's car or taking them home until a relationship has been established. It's a big, scary world out there and a bit of circumspection could make all the difference.

The introduction may be a bit contrived, but if things are looking positive, try to establish a real-life context for your relationship as soon as possible. You can get to know someone over the phone and online but it is preferable to see them in their everyday setting, relating to friends, family and colleagues and you in many varied situations.

Questions

You have met, you have fallen in love and you are considering marriage. What questions relate specifically to your situation, and have you addressed them carefully? Here are some suggestions for things to look at:

1. Have I had opportunity to really get to know this person? Have I met their family and friends? Have I spent a good amount of time with them, and do I trust they are who they tell me they are? (It is very important that you answer these in the affirmative before going ahead with plans to get married.)
2. What are the 'non-negotiable' qualities on my list? Does this person have them?
3. Am I happy to tell people how we met?

8

Take Two:
Engagement after Divorce

Nobody gets married with the intention of divorcing a few years down the line. There might be those who see divorce as a safety net; knowing it is an option might make the first steps out onto the tightrope a little less fearsome. There might be those who see it as an emergency exit for use in case the fires of love burn out. But for most people, 'till death do us part' means just that, and the very concept of divorce is a long way from their minds as they turn smiling and confident to wave at their guests having been pronounced husband and wife.

Tragically, many marriages do end in divorce. Stumbling from such catastrophic wreckage, there are those who feel they are injured beyond repair. The pain and damage resulting from the severing of two individuals who have become one is real and lasting. But sometimes a second chance at getting it right presents itself. How is it different this time around, and what are the lasting consequences of the first attempt?

I should say at the outset that I am not going to even dip a tentative toe into the muddy waters of the theology of divorce and remarriage. You will have to do your homework on that somewhere else, and reach your own conclusions. There are many good books written on the subject, and you could talk to your church leaders and mature Christian friends as you wrestle through what you believe. For now, let's focus on one particular couple who have made it through this minefield without too many explosions going off, and who are a beacon of hope for those disillusioned by marriage.

Markku and Leah

I met Leah when I first went to Canada, in 1996. My parents were teaching a course at Regent College, Vancouver and the whole family joined them for the school Easter holidays. Before we got there they gave us brief character sketches of the students they had in their class, including a duo they had dubbed 'The Heavenly Twins'. Leah is half of the heavenly twins. She and her husband Markku generously agreed to let me plunder their story, which I'm sure you'll agree is a good one. Are you sitting comfortably? Then I shall begin.

Things fell apart for Markku and his first wife three years into their marriage. It seems she struggled with profound issues of identity in the year prior to their separation, and shortly after leaving the relationship became involved with someone else. It was a horrible, painful time, and the process of divorcing was as messy and destructive as divorce frequently is. No one would choose to write this eventuality into the script of their life. However, God can always turn a desert into a place of springs, and at twenty-seven Markku had much unseen joy ahead of him. It was also this crisis that kick-started his faith, present in childhood but left behind in subsequent years. He writes:

> In the midst of my rejection, grief and loss I turned to the only one I knew who would never reject me. During these days I lived in North Vancouver and would spend a lot of time outside walking and running in Lynn Canyon. I vividly recall standing on the bridge over the canyon wanting to end my life. I couldn't of course, because I felt loved by God and by my family. But in a way I did jump off that bridge – I prayed and gave my life to Jesus. My life wasn't my own anymore.

A year later, he and Leah met for the first time since his divorce. They had been acquaintances while studying for Masters Degrees and Leah had heard of his marriage breakdown through mutual friends, and had been praying for him. Now they were both part of a weekend work team at Pioneer Pacific Camp, on one of Canada's gulf islands, and they began to get to know each other on a deeper level. During the weekend, Leah was surprised at how often they seemed to bump into each other, but appreciated the chances they had to talk. Both were nursing broken hearts, as Leah was at the end of a relationship she had thought was leading to marriage, and they intuitively understood each other's vulnerability. As she was leaving Canada to teach in Lithuania two months later, Leah had no thought of anything other than friendship, but as she found out later, Markku was having all sorts of thoughts. They had begun the night before he arrived at the island, when having been told by friends that Leah was to be a part of the group, he felt inexplicably intrigued and excited at the prospect of seeing her, to the extent that he was unable to sleep. On the ferry over to the island after his broken night, he had an epiphany of sorts (which the pragmatic Leah attributes to his sleep deprivation!) in which he had a sudden and clear sense that despite the grim reality of his divorce, his future was going to be very bright and that Leah was somehow to be involved. If she had had an inkling of this she might not have been so surprised to bump into him around every corner that weekend!

They exchanged email addresses when they said their goodbyes and Leah headed off to the other side of the world. Markku had decided not to write to her unless she wrote to him first; fortunately he had been included on her mass mailing list – all the encouragement he needed to strike up a correspondence. They wrote back and forth in a sporadic fashion for some time, until Markku was spurred into action by a chance conversation with a friend. Over home-made granola and coffee, or whatever they had for breakfast as good Canadians, this friend asked casually, 'Do you think I should marry Leah Potts?' Markku's answer ran along the lines of 'Leah seems like a fine girl' but inside he was a bit taken aback, as he himself had been thinking of marrying Leah and had no inclination to gallantly step aside and allow the competition to take the lead. This conversation seems a little strange, so we'll let Leah put it into some perspective:

> To set the record straight, this other fellow wasn't at all in love with me – he had the Asian model of marriage in mind: start with a simmer and bring the pot to a boil rather than the Western model which starts at a boil. Furthermore, he's not really the marrying type and I don't think he was really serious.

Furthermore, I would have said 'no' should such a proposition have been volleyed my way.

So let's not spare a moment's pity for this young man, but rather be grateful to him for his cameo role in our story. As he exits stage left, he has provided the necessary impetus for our hero to spring into action – a healthy panic at signs of competition on the horizon. Shortly thereafter, perhaps having washed up the granola bowls and topped up his coffee, he dispatched an email confessing 'a bit of a crush' and off they went into the land of long distance dating.

Leah returned to Canada for a few weeks the following summer, and they led a week-long kayak trip together around the gulf islands, giving each of them the chance to see what the other looked like after seven days of not washing – a great test for those awkward early days of a relationship! But also a pretty good context in which to observe the other person interacting with a range of people, dealing with stress and demonstrating leadership and wilderness survival skills. That they somehow managed to impress one another under these conditions is staggering! By the time Leah had to leave for the next school year in Lithuania they had met both sets of parents – no mean feat, given that Leah's lived in Arizona and Markku's in the interior of British Columbia – and knew things were serious. Markku went to Lithuania for a week that term, and marriage became a very likely prospect.

I am never one to shrink from probing, intrusive questions, and so I asked Leah how she had felt about Markku being a divorcee. Her reply was gracious and sane, and along the lines of all of us having experiences that leave us a little bit more broken, and this was just one of those for Markku. It was important to both of them that significant healing had occurred from each of their previous break ups before they got together, and this had truly happened. Maybe the process was made easier by their uncanny compatibility: they shared a common outlook on spirituality, politics, recreation and ministry. They wanted the same things in life and enjoyed being together.

Despite the pain he had gone through, Markku was still committed to the ideal of marriage and had always hoped he would remarry at some stage. He had gone to counselling, done lots of reading, become part of a thriving church community and done his best to face his hurt in the hope of being able to move on. His relationship with Leah was part of the process of healing, but also threw up plenty of fear, and it took him a lot of courage to initiate their engagement. God, having a sublime sense of humour and understanding of what Markku's particular needs were, seems to have laid on all sorts of quirky encouragements and signs to prompt him along the way. In his words:

> The most hilarious one was this day that I was at work in front of the computer occasionally checking email and experiencing some cyber anxiety about emails to and from Leah. Anywho [that's a Canadian-ism not a typo!] I was praying about the anxiety and thinking of Leah in Lithuania. The radio was on playing soft rock and this song came on with the chorus – 'Lithuania, Lithuania...' How random was that? I took it as a sign of encouragement to pursue Leah and felt a real peace in it all.

Their engagement happened in two parts. Part one was over the telephone. Having not heard from Markku in a few days, and this being in the dark ages of eye-wateringly expensive international calling, when he did call at a non-pre-arrranged time Leah feared it was to break up with her. The truth was, he had been investigating possible dates available at her ideal wedding venue and had discovered there were only three spots left for the following summer. He would need to move fast if they were to secure one, and this of course, entailed getting engaged.

Picture the scene. It is 8 a.m., at the front desk of Karklu Dorm, Klaipeda, Lithuania, location of the one telephone in the building. Leah, slightly puffed from her swift descent down five flights of stairs, and still wearing her dressing gown, takes the call in the midst of a river of students heading off to class in long woollen coats:

Markku: So I called Cecil Green College and they only have three places left.
Leah: Oh.
Markku: So, should I book one?
Leah: Uh, sure I guess so.
Markku: So, we'd be getting married then. Do you want to get married?
Leah: Yeah, sure, that sounds good.
Markku: Okay, talk to you soon.
[Click.]

If this gives you the impression that Markku is not a romantic kind of person, let me quickly disabuse you of that notion. The engagement, part two, must surely strike dread into the hearts of young men with marital aspirations everywhere. Maybe, if this includes you, you could rip this page out of the book, make sure your girlfriend never sees it, and steal the idea. I just know she'd be impressed. When Leah returned home for Christmas, he picked her up from the airport, cooked her a seafood feast, lit a fire and gave her a welcome home present: Elizabeth Barrett Browning's *Sonnets from the Portuguese*. On the inside cover he had inscribed his proposal, which shall remain private, and then he had cut out a heart-shaped hole in each page up to the poem 'How Shall I Love Thee, Let Me Count the Ways' where he had tied the ring. Of course she melted into his arms and agreed to become his wife, even if the ring wasn't *quite* what she wanted and the fish stew was *slightly* on the salty side: we are talking real life here!

Decision Time (Again...)

Getting through life without becoming tarnished by corrosive cynicism is a major endeavour. One year at a work Christmas party I spent some time in idle chit-chat with a co-worker, as one does at these functions, and discovered in the course of our conversation that her journey through life had taught her some lessons: all men are ruled by their groins, your children are just out to manipulate you and take your money, and success as a woman depends on plastic surgery and aggression. Listening to her, my mulled wine began to taste bitter and my seasonal cheer started to droop around the edges.

Our philosophy of life is formed partially through what has happened to us – our beliefs and judgments of how things happen and what they mean are constantly being re-evaluated in the light of our everyday reality. For example, we might believe our home is a secure place until it is broken into and all our possessions are taken, and then we adjust our expectation that we can control who comes in and out and maybe become a bit paranoid for a time. We could let that one incident override all our previous observations about how the house thing works, or we could, once we calm down and replace our belongings with new and better ones, simply add some more security features and remind ourselves that houses are mostly quite secure. (By the way – when you replace your stuff, don't put all the boxes out in front of your house. Some friends of mine at university made this mistake and had the whole lot stolen a second time.) So how does this relate to marriage? Well, some basic assumptions are challenged when a person gets divorced. Markku could have drawn the following conclusions based on his experience:

- Marriage does not last forever.
- You can't trust a woman to be faithful.
- You have no control over what happens to you. You are at the mercy of unreliable people who will hurt you given the chance.
- Life is not going to turn out well for you unless you protect yourself from intimacy.

Deciding to remarry is a decision to fly in the face of the reality you might have been presented with, and to choose to believe that what you have gone through does not represent a general truth. Markku's first wife might have been unfaithful, but he managed to contain that fact to the specific person and situation and not apply it universally. It is important to dig out the conclusions that could be drawn from an experience of divorce and address them before bringing them into a new relationship. This means heading into the heart of the tornado of anger, hurt and disillusionment and perhaps even being swept up in it for a time, terrifying as that may seem. It is better than running from it, never knowing when it will land and rip the roof off your house.

Being able to forgive is an essential element in the healing process, and as Markku says, 'Without coming to this point of true forgiveness, I don't think it is possible to be in a healthy second marriage.' This also involves forgiving yourself. Most breakdowns in marriages are to some extent the responsibility of both partners, and both will need to accept their share of the blame and then forgive themselves for what went wrong. Understanding what happened will also enable any changes to be made the next time around and thus make it seem less about random chance and more about controllable actions.

Your Past: My Past?

Very few of us come to marriage with no relational baggage, and for those that do, that lack of baggage can be its own kind of baggage. A person who has been single until they meet 'The One' might wonder why romantic relationships had eluded them thus far, or bring unrealistic hopes of perfection to the relationship when it finally happens. These days, we tend to marry a bit later on in life, having gone through several relationships of varying duration and intensity, and each one will have left an imprint on who we are. We will have memories, photographs and associations with places and times that bring an old relationship to mind – and to some degree we will carry these people with us through our whole lives. In the person you have fallen in love with, the presence of the past can be hard to accept. I remember sitting on a big rock in the dark at the beach with Shawn shortly after we began dating, while we both sketched out in deliberately vague detail our relationship histories for each other, even at that early stage feeling an acute sense of sadness that we had experienced anything of this sort with anyone other than each other. When you are first in love with someone, you want to be everything to them, past and future and present. But we must make peace with the way things are. We have to cut any attachments we might still be holding onto; if we exchange Anglican marriage vows, this will be part of the 'forsaking all others' we promise to do. We have to forgive ourselves for having given more fully of ourselves than we ought to have outside marriage, physically, spiritually and emotionally, and we have to forgive the people who broke our hearts.

Not only do we need to leave aside our own past, but we need to leave aside our husband or wife's past too. This might be a girl-thing, but it is possible to cause ourselves exquisite pain by indulging in horrible daydreams about what our beloved shared with someone else before we came along, and wallowing in the fact that they were once not ours. This is not a great idea: they need to move on and you need to move on too.

Needless to say, all the issues of past relationships are far more acutely present if the past relationship was a marriage. There are layers and layers of complexity to work through here, much more so if there are children involved, and I imagine there are all sorts of painful moments that jump out at you when you least expect it.

However, with self-discipline and patience, it is totally possible to keep the past from dominating or dictating to the present.

Aftertastes

I know all sorts of people who are in happy, thriving second marriages. They are determined to make it work, they know the pitfalls and the dangers and they take them seriously, they have tackled their problems with tenacity and courage. They are amazed and grateful to be given another chance and do not take a minute of marital harmony for granted. The cold weather front is moving off and the outlook is sunny and warm. But life being what it is this side of heaven, there will still be lingering pain to contend with. Markku says candidly:

> There is brokenness that I will experience for the rest of my life. It's been over ten years and I still have random moments of grief and sadness even though I'm completely happy in our marriage and feel like my life now is such a gift. Usually every year around the anniversary of the separation I go through four–six weeks of depression...

I mention this not to cruelly undermine your fragile optimism, but to encourage you not to despair when you hit these times of sorrow and regret.

Questions

1. Do you feel you understand what went wrong in your first marriage, and have you taken responsibility for your part in it?
2. Have you given yourself proper time to grieve and be angry and forgive?
3. Have you got a good community to support you in your new marriage?

9

Conversion

I don't know if you have ever seen a person go through a religious conversion from close up. I have witnessed several people becoming Christians, and as a fellow Christian I find this something to rejoice over – I watch the changes in their lives and characters with fascination and delight, and I experience my friendship with them deepen as we gain a whole new world of commonality. Depending on where you are sitting though, this conversion business could be seen very differently. If it happens to your boyfriend or girlfriend, it can be extremely worrying and even threatening. You liked them the way they were, and you don't want to see them changing. You don't appreciate their different priorities, especially when they involve shifting you down a few notches on the totem pole. You suddenly realize that a whole bunch of relative strangers seem to understand them better than you do, and they keep taking them off to meetings and events that cut into your sacred couple time. You feel they have become judgmental about your moral fibre and have an agenda to get you to change. Your previously stable relationship hangs in the balance, and its survival seems to depend on what you think about God, previously the domain of tipsy late night philosophising, the conclusions of which were forgotten in the queasiness of the following morning's fry-up. Worst of all, they might start denying you sex. Aaaaaagh!

Or it could be that you like the transformation. They might have become less selfish, more likely to offer to make the tea, more forgiving of your foibles and grouchiness. You may have wanted to explore Christianity yourself, but just needed the impetus. Either way, conversion is going to shake things up profoundly, and your relationship may or may not survive it.

It takes courage and integrity to pursue spiritual truth in the knowledge that it may pull you away from the person who means the most to you in the world. I have seen many people weigh up the risk and choose to walk away from God – it can seem too great a sacrifice. There are several possible outcomes of becoming a Christian when dating someone who is not a Christian, and one of those is that the relationship will end. That is a scary and unpleasant prospect, especially if you are planning on getting married someday. Another outcome is that both people will become Christians. This will still be fairly disruptive, as we can see from Sarah and Dave's story, but it may well lead to a deeper, stronger and more fulfilling relationship in the long run.

Sarah and Dave

Sarah and I met next to a heaving dessert table and thereby discovered a common passion. To put our serendipitous meeting into context, I had just started a three-month stint as an au pair in North London, and the family I was working for had sent me up to their church's newcomers' event so I could meet some potential friends. Sarah had just arrived back in London after a year of travelling the world, and was also in the market for new friends. Now, years later, we are godparents to each other's children, and still enjoy chatting over an indulgent pudding or two.

For me that autumn was all about chasing around after three small children, trying to keep a big family home in a tolerably tidy state, bolting out of London to somewhere rural every weekend I could and spending time with Sarah in a variety of pubs in and around Muswell Hill. For Sarah, it was mostly about Dave.

What I didn't know, standing at the dessert table that evening, was that it was a fairly new thing to find Sarah at a church event of any kind, even one with so many puddings to choose from. The year on the ship had been one of monumental change in her character, attitudes and general direction: in short, she had undergone a dramatic conversion. She was full of the enthusiasm of the new Christian, but she was also having to face the fact that the change she had undergone was causing major disruption to her previously blissful relationship with her boyfriend.

Sarah and Dave had met while she was at art college in Brighton and he was doing teacher training. After a few months of friendship, she had driven him up to Newcastle to take his stuff to store at his parents' house. The car conked out in Doncaster, which to many would seem a bit of a drag, but to them was a fun adventure. We can deduce from this just how smitten they must have been (or possibly how dull their everyday lives were – but knowing them I'd have to go for the first, kinder, interpretation). The next day, having revived the sickly car and escaped the tourist trap of Doncaster, they went to a Pogues concert. The concert was of the sort that attracts the kind of fans who fill their mouths with beer and spray each other with it. Nice. After the concert they went for a walk in a thunderstorm (perhaps to wash off the beer/saliva mix) and had their first kiss. They fell significantly and dizzily in love with each other from that moment.

After they had been together for a year, Sarah made the decision to join Operation Mobilisation and spend a year on one of their ships. This is an organization that is primarily oriented towards evangelism, so fairly obviously a Christian outfit, but she saw them as a way of seeing the world and broadening her experience, and she managed to get accepted on the programme by telling a few little white lies ('Yes, I go to Church every Sunday – praise the Lord!'). As much as she loved Dave, settling down was not yet on her agenda.

As thrilling as the expedition had seemed in prospect, her first day on the ship saw her sitting on the toilet crying her eyes out, and praying, 'God, who are you? What is this all about?' She had never felt so alone or so miserable. After this significant toilet-moment (We've all had one, haven't we?) she started to read the Bible, and for the first time it made sense to her. She couldn't get enough of it, and it began to change her.

Meanwhile, back in Brighton, Dave was dealing with unruly brats on his teaching placement, incessant rain and a hovel of a bachelor pad to live in. He ran up £400 pounds on a phone bill in the first three months Sarah was away. The ship was docked off the coast of southern India at Christmas and Dave came out to stay, much to his dismay, in a separate cabin from his long-lost girlfriend. He thought she had gone a bit mad – the sea air and the hot house (hot boat?) of religious fervour had obviously been unhealthy for her. It worried him.

Somehow they staggered on through the next months apart. Sarah was under a lot of pressure to break up with him from her new friends on the ship, but never felt this was the right thing to do. Instead, she prayed for him day and night, and found to her surprise that Dave was beginning to report some interesting developments – first he met a Christian at work, and then he went to Church... all very improbable. She had to conclude her prayers were being answered.

At the end of the year, she flew to France to meet up with her family on holiday and Dave joined them there. They had a horrible reunion, not helped by the fact that she had overslept and was an hour late to meet him at Grenoble train station. With things by now so tense and uncertain between them, they decided to hitch to the south. This would at least give them something to do other than sitting around in awkward silence.

Back in London, they tried to keep things going. Dave had begun to pursue God in earnest by this point, but Sarah felt more and more pressure from her church friends to break up with him, and eventually came to believe it was what she had to do. Days and days of tears followed, dark days in which even puddings offered no solace, and then a couple of months during which they had no contact. It was horrible seeing her so sad and missing him so much, but I suppose I assumed she had done the right thing and in time would start feeling better.

They were still going to the same church, but it was enormous and they could easily be at the same service without seeing each other. One evening, Sarah caught sight of him on the other side of the packed building, and knew instantly something was different about him. They found each other at the end and Dave told her he had made the decision to become a Christian that weekend.

By then I had left to spend eight months in Zimbabwe working in a rural primary school. Our mail was eagerly awaited and arrived haphazardly at any given time of day in the grubby hands of small boys running out of the bush – we never found out how or where they got hold of it. One day I was sitting outside my concrete hut when one of the said grubby boys delivered a fat missive from Sarah with news that not only had she got back together with Dave, but that they were engaged and were going to get married in a few short months and would like me to be a bridesmaid. Apart from the fact she would not now be coming to join me for a month of travel, I was extremely happy for them. Whether I would have been so happy if I had known what I would be wearing for the wedding is another question: Sarah is still apologizing! The letter explained that shortly after Dave had become a Christian, they had walked out of church one morning, and turned to each other simultaneously with the question 'When are we going to do this then?' on their lips.

If any of you think this is less than romantic as proposals go, the story of the ring more than compensates. Dave had trained as a teacher but was trying to avoid teaching (something to do with those unruly 'Brats of Brighton' perhaps) and was honing his skills in the area of plastic bag manufacture. The plastic bag factory began to see a great deal of him over the following weeks as he did nightshifts and overtime to save up for the ring Sarah had spotted on Regent Street, a beautiful pearl surrounded by twelve diamonds. One evening as they were walking along the embankment, he got down on one knee and produced this costly treasure – declaring his hope that whenever she looked at it she would be reminded of just how much he loved her.

Marrying a Christian

Sarah and Dave, although they had their ups and downs to negotiate, were very fortunate to become Christians together. They have a marriage based on a shared spiritual paradigm – they are both seeking to know God better and live their lives jointly and individually to that end. Whatever struggles they have had, they have been able to turn to God for help and strength to love each other. However, plenty of people find that only one in the couple comes to faith. For a couple who aren't yet married, one of the first considerations to face in this situation is whether a marriage should still take place.

I wrestled personally with the issue of whether a Christian should marry someone who wasn't a Christian when I was nineteen. My first serious boyfriend was not a Christian and yet in so many ways seemed my ideal match. We talked about marriage a lot, but as hard as I tried, I could not get around the obstacle of our differing beliefs. We ended up parting company and I have never doubted that was the right thing to do, painful as it was at the time. I know there will be people reading this who are wrestling over this same issue, and I don't mean to lay down the law and make you feel worse than you do, but here are some of the reasons that I took the decision I did.

Firstly, I had been praying about what to do and I felt more clearly than I have ever done before or since that God spoke to me and asked me to walk away as a matter of obedience. I do believe that if you want to follow God and hear his voice that he will help you know what the right thing to do is. I have not had many times when it has been that loud and persistent but I do think we should always try and listen to what God might want to tell us.

Sensing God's intentions as I prayed was the subjective part of my decision. Objectively, I saw more and more possible complications arising for us in the future if we continued down such separate paths. The Christian life, lived wholeheartedly, is going to impact how you spend your money, what you do with your time, how you relate to people, how you make decisions, raise your children, deal with suffering and so on. Marriage needs a core of agreed values or it turns into a perpetual battle ground. If I had married this boyfriend, we would have been pulling in different directions and trying to impose ways of thinking on the other that were foreign or unnatural. Over time, to keep the peace, I imagine one or other of us would have been moulded to a more convenient shape, and I had to admit that could have been me: I would essentially be risking the quality and integrity of my faith for a human relationship.

I was already a Christian when the relationship began, but for some people, one half of the couple becomes a Christian part way through, and this can be really disruptive. If they are already married, it is clearly the right thing to stay married. But if they are not, it can throw up some very complex difficulties to deal with. The main one will be that you are not the same person you were before, whether this is dramatically apparent or not. Your boyfriend or girlfriend will probably be very unnerved by this change and will have to get to know you all over again. Then your ideas about marriage might change – it might become more important, and more permanent as a concept. You might decide you should stop having sex until you have made that commitment. And it might become very important to you that the other person share your faith, which could be very threatening to them. Whatever happens, something will. It is not going to stay the same.

What Conversion does to Attitudes to Marriage

My friends Amanda and Chris had been living together for several months, and although they considered themselves very committed to each other, they did not have plans to marry in the immediate future. When they both came to faith, they found their attitude towards marriage had changed significantly. Having made a lifelong commitment to God, the commitment of marriage was not nearly as daunting. They had new assurance that they would be able to keep their vows, with a stronger moral code structuring their lives, and the Holy Spirit to help them. They felt it was no longer right to live together while being unmarried and yet didn't want to live apart for longer than absolutely necessary. They wanted God's blessing on their relationship, and the acknowledgment and support of their community of faith behind them. And so they moved into separate accommodation, got engaged and shortly thereafter were married.

I do not intend to suggest that marriage is not held as a highly valued institution by people with no religious convictions – it very often is. But a conversion can be a catalyst for moving the process along, and can bring people to the point of being ready and willing to get married earlier than they might have before.

Questions

You may well disagree with me that it is important to marry a fellow Christian. I know plenty of people who do, and this is something you will have to figure out. These questions are going to assume that both you and your boyfriend or girlfriend have become Christians, and are now thinking about marriage:

1. Are you both secure in your faith? Would you continue in your Christian commitment if the relationship came to an end?
2. What changes do you see in each other as a result of coming to faith?
3. What, if anything, is different about how you understand marriage since becoming Christians? What do you understand to be God's vision and design for marriage?
4. Have you prayed about your decision, alone and together? Have you sought the advice of mature Christians? Have you considered doing some sort of formal marriage preparation?

10

Arranged Marriages

My dad rather fancies himself as a matchmaker, and takes dubious credit for a number of the more successful marriages of his friends and acquaintances. In reality his involvement usually consists of whispering to Mum that so and so and so and so would make a great couple. Not exactly wresting the arm of fate, shall we say. In the case of an extremely good idea that has not caught on with the individuals concerned, he might go as far as to engineer occasions when they can spend time together and have opportunity to spot their obvious compatibility, but really he takes a hands-off approach. Anything more directive would seem strange and probably inappropriate seen through western eyes. And if he had tried to organize his daughters' love lives in any way other than by strong suggestion, a tactic he is not afraid to use, we would be outraged, and quite rightly so. It is not the way we do things these days, at least not in the cultures I have been exposed to. So, when I came across a number of people who were happily allowing their families to organize spouses for them, I was fascinated, and maybe you will be too.

133

Asha and Raji

Last year, the National Society for Epilepsy, my place of employment, had a recruitment drive for nurses in India, and as a result I got to work alongside some very interesting people. I soon learnt, as we chatted our way through shifts, that most of them were expecting arranged marriages. Well, this was very intriguing, and so I asked multitudes of probing questions which they patiently and graciously answered. The picture that emerged was different from the one I had had in my head. I am sure there is variation across regions and religions, so I should point out to the knowledgeable that these girls are from relatively well off Christian families in the southern state of Kerala.

The sense of family honour and obligation is very strong among the girls that I talked to. I wanted to know what would happen if they met someone in the course of their studies or travel and sorted out their own marriage partner, thus entering into what they call a 'love marriage'. The very suggestion of such impropriety provoked wide-eyed horror among them. This behaviour would bring unbearable disgrace upon their families and they would not consider it. One of them, named Kanchan, explained that as her father had died when she was a child, she felt an extra burden to behave honourably so her mother would not be seen to have brought up her child badly.

The search for a suitable husband is a long process. For my nursing friends, the start of the search begins when they themselves decide they are ready. Although compared to a western style of courtship they have little say in who they marry, there are still aspects over which they retain control. So they tell their families when they feel the time is right, which is likely to be when they are around twenty-five years old, and only then will the families put the word out, either through an agency with this specific function, or through their personal networks, or even through the newspaper. They will be looking for someone with the same religious background, a good family and respectable career prospects. Details of prospective husbands will begin to come in, and the girls will assess the potential of each (and whether they like the look of the photo, although this seems lower down the list of priorities than I would have expected from my own, superficial perspective). If they express interest in any of the suitors then a visit will be arranged between the two families. Tea will be served, and a cagey interview carried out to ascertain the suitability of the match. The girl will be left alone with the boy for a few minutes, and on the strength of this meeting, she will tell her parents if she wants to marry him or not. There is no obligation to settle for the first option, or even the tenth; they continue to set up these meetings for as long as it takes to find someone who they are happy with. After agreement is given, a date for an engagement party will be fixed, dowries decided on, and arrangements for the marriage ceremony set in motion. The couple may be able to speak over the phone, but they will not meet again until their official engagement, and they will probably not be alone again until they are married.

During the year we worked together, one of the girls, Asha, went through this process and agreed to let me put her story in writing. I found it intriguing to watch her fall in love with a relative stranger as the months unfolded, speaking about her intended with breathy intensity, carrying her mobile around with her as though it were a treasured Chihuahua puppy and cooing over his photo, a small and slightly blurry portrait of a stiffly-posed man in front of a house – the most handsome man in the world according to her. It blew apart any ideas I had of arranged marriages being the source of bitter night-time tears or dreary resignation. This was as much a love story as any I have come across, and somehow sweeter for its innocence and novelty.

It all began last March when Asha went back to India for a month's holiday, having decided now was the right time to think about marriage. Her family arranged for several men to visit the house with their families but she didn't find any of them particularly to her liking, so she made a suggestion to her parents. This is another way in which the process can be managed in order to involve a fair amount of pro-activity on the part of the bride-to-be. Her brother had brought a friend home on her previous visit, and she remembered that at the time she had thought he seemed pleasant. Raji's background and prospects were deemed suitable, so enquiries were made and events set in motion. During their ten minutes of privacy she asked him about his interests and what he wanted to do in life, and he asked her similar things, and their answers must have been mutually agreeable because they both informed their families later on that day that they would like to get married.

She came back to England and continued life as a nurse, but with a growing attachment to that phone and a noticeable sparkle in her eyes. I would catch her singing to herself and smiling for no apparent reason, and generally appearing unbelievably happy. It seemed as though a rather calculated and cranial choice of husband had become an affair of the heart, recognisable the world over as love.

The time eventually came for the marriage to take place. With great excitement Asha took annual leave and returned home to seal the deal. The official engagement was far, far removed from the scenario we are used to here in England, with the man and the woman exchanging private promises in a secluded location and then bursting forth to announce what they have decided to the world. All of Asha's relatives came to stay at her family home for the occasion. A beautician came to the house to decorate her hands with Mehendi, intricate powder designs. Her female relatives, with great exuberance and noisy festivity, helped her dress in a home-made maroon sarara, a top/skirt/shawl ensemble, and tame her contrary hair. She was decked out in the gold bangles and chains which were to form part of her dowry. At eleven o' clock the whole party drove to the church, to be greeted by the great throng of Raji and his family, friends and well-wishers, along with those in the vicinity drawn to the celebratory mass of people. Raji and Asha walked into the sanctuary leading the colourful crowd, and there prayers were said and they were asked publicly if they were willing to marry each other. Having given consent, they processed back to Asha's home where the families finalized wedding plans, sealed the matter of the dowry and set a date to go shopping for wedding clothing the next week. The actual marriage ceremony happened seven days later.

Expectations

At different points in my pre-Shawn existence, I would survey my choices of boyfriend so far, and wonder if I should give up the decision of who to marry to someone wiser and more discerning. I occasionally thought about who my parents might choose for me if I gave the matter over into their hands. When we lived in the field study centre in Portugal they seemed to know a lot of musty-smelling birdwatchers, and I assumed it would have to be one of them. I liked them all, and even had crushes on the better looking and more fragrant of the bunch, but as marriage material, something wasn't quite right. Probably the birdwatching thing. And realistically, much as I trust my parents and their investment in wanting the best for me, I wouldn't *really* have let them find me a husband. I think this is mostly because I have grown up with the expectation that I would meet someone, fall in love and organize my own future with that person with extremely limited outside involvement. Asha, on the other hand, expected that like her parents, her grandparents, her great grandparents and all her respectable contemporaries, she would have her marriage arranged. She never gave the slightest impression that she wished things to be different. There are cases in which marriage is forced upon unwilling participants; I can't imagine anyone being particularly thrilled at this – especially if they are expected to be a second, third or fourth wife, if they find the prospective groom repulsive, or know him to be cruel. If they happen to have fallen in love with someone else, or are so young they don't understand what's going on, it would be a tragic occurrence. Asha knew she would not have to marry before she was ready, and that she had the all powerful veto. Her girlish dreams of romance would have involved that ten minutes alone with her potential groom, and the gradual, steady involvement of emotion that followed. Nothing in her current situation was less than what she was expecting.

A Great Cloud of Witnesses

In our society, we have almost total freedom to decide for ourselves who we marry. I say almost, because there are still some restrictions: they have to be over sixteen, unmarried, not a close relative and human. (British tabloids reported a wedding recently between a London business woman and a dolphin in Eilat, Israel, but you can't believe everything you read in the tabloids.) Despite this freedom, we don't have a very good success rate. There are a plethora of possible explanations, but I think part of it could relate again to expectations: we hope to find an ideal that doesn't exist and then it is all too easy, legally anyway, to cut losses and start the search all over again. So would it be a good idea to tighten up divorce legislation and adopt a moderated form of the arranged marriage set up? Honestly, I couldn't see it working when we have all got so used to our autonomy. But there could be a case for greater accountability to our wider communities and more involvement of family and friends. This already happens to an extent: the subtle introductions manoeuvred at dinner parties, the church house group that caters to the single demographic, the freely given assessments dished out after first introducing a new boyfriend or girlfriend to those close to you. Maybe we should consider giving more weight to this informally given guidance? My youngest sister would want to protest loudly at this suggestion. As the last unmarried member of the family, she is the focus of intense observation and comment – we are not easily satisfied and so far her boyfriends have provoked loud protestations. The poor girl has a lot to contend with, not to mention any brave suitor she is foolish enough to present to the panel of judges. Of course, of prime importance is that she should know for herself whether the boyfriend is marriage material, but is the approval of the family helpful or even relevant? Our families and friends, hopefully, know us well, and have our best interests at heart. They will not be contending with the crazy chemical disruption of love and will possibly be able to have a helpful objective perspective to offer on our chances of long-term happiness. A friend of mine whose marriage sadly didn't survive, tells how her closest friends all admitted they had had grave reservations and worries about the marriage, but these only came out once the ink had dried on the divorce papers. She wishes they had spoken up earlier, however horrible it would have been to hear at the time.

The other side of this is that your family and friends could have iffy motivations for wanting you to marry or not to marry a certain person – they could be dazzled by healthy finances, or like the fact that the chap lives in the same village as them and won't take you off to the other side of the world. But more crucially, you are the one who will be married to this person, and you are the one who will live day in day out with them, not your family and friends. Listen carefully to the advice you are given, weigh it up, and then you must make your own decision, at least in our culture and our time.

Two Dates or Less

I am deeply indebted to a book entitled, *'How to Know If Someone is Worth Pursuing in Two Dates or Less'*. My husband got his hands on it after dating a girl for five years and in the time it took him to read the book he realized she was not the girl for him and promptly ended the relationship. Her loss: my gain. The part of Asha and Raji's story that I found hardest to relate to was the bit where she had ten minutes with him in order to decide whether to marry him or not. How could this possibly be enough? In our society we are encouraged to know the product inside out before buying – the majority live together in a pseudo-marriage set up in order to test run all aspects of compatibility while there is still an easy way out. Even committed Christians will try to do the sensible thing and have a long relationship, seeing each other in a variety of contexts and situations and company before deeming it wise to exchange vows. If we are trying to eliminate the possibility of failure, our divorce rate shows us our approach is not working. Asha felt she could sign up for a future with this man after their brief encounter because she knew his pedigree, his background, his qualifications, and liked his face well enough. So I don't really think it would work for romantic westerners, even though it does seem much simpler, and seems to work perfectly well for many cultures. What some of us could take and learn from this though, is to be a bit less melodramatic about getting married. It is a perfectly normal thing to do – it has been done throughout human history and across the world, and maybe in space, who knows? There could be alien marriage ceremonies taking place every few seconds. We know we won't end up with an ideal person, since there is no such being on our planet, and once a few fundamentals are in place, maybe we should calm down and take the leap without having all the risks eliminated and all the boxes ticked.

Questions

If you are in the process of entering an arranged marriage, I wish you every happiness, and all God's wisdom as you take this step. I hope these questions will be helpful to those who are taking matters into their own hands.

1. Do you have people in your life who know you well and whose wisdom you trust? Who are they? Have you sought their blessing on your relationship and given them permission to speak honestly to you about any hesitations they may have?
2. In what situations do you spend time with your significant other? Have people you both know had the chance to see you interacting as a couple?
3. Do you have a common community to which you are accountable?

11

Sensible Sausages

I wonder if parents of little girls look at them playing innocently on the swings, and start to daydream about their future. Playground life can't be all that exciting for adults, so I'm sure that between pushes, the mind has ample opportunity to wander. As she swings back and forth, back and forth, they might imagine her bringing down the house as angel number two in the school nativity play, swanning through academic challenges, graduating at last as a fully qualified vet (she's always been so good with the guinea pigs) and now, the real tear jerker, walking down the aisle towards a blurry figure at the altar. What hopes and fears would a parent feel as they contemplate that far off day and that yet to be revealed person? Perhaps that the relationship would make their daughter happy; that the man be trustworthy, kind, hardworking; that he would see their daughter for who she is and love her wholeheartedly. They might fear that she would marry someone she didn't really know, that she would be caught up in dresses and cake and flowers and not properly examine the enormity of what marriage means, that she might fuse her fortunes with a glaringly unsuitable partner and become lost to them and perhaps herself. Let's shake our parents out of their playground reverie and lead them in some relaxing breathing techniques, before they head home to make jam sandwiches (no crusts please daddy) and empty the dishwasher.

We have come to the category of relationships which is deeply reassuring to parents of prospective brides and grooms: the sensible sort, which ticks all the right boxes, follows a sedate and timely course, and is looked on by all as the obvious and right thing to be happening between these two lovely people. I really don't mean to suggest that if your story doesn't match up at all the key points that something has gone wrong. But let's look at what would make a relationship seem particularly right, especially from a protective parent's point of view.

Lennie and Dan

Lennie (christened Helen, in case you were wondering) is one of my sister's university housemates. Beth, my sister, is at the university where I studied, so visits to see her are always a bit of a trip down memory lane. Actually, memory alley would be more apt for the part of town infested by students: think broken glass, rotting kebabs, mouldy mattresses and neon club fliers by the thousand clogging up the gutters – studying and good citizenship don't always go hand in hand! The house occupied by my sister, Lennie, and two other girls however, is a haven of hygiene, mood lighting and fresh vegetables in the midst of this dereliction. There are terracotta tiles in the kitchen, framed pictures on the sitting room walls, and a shocking lack of all things mouldy, broken and mismatched.

Lennie arrived at university two weeks into a relationship with Dan, a policeman working in London.

The stereotypical outcome would have been for Lennie to have pined for him horribly for the whole of her first term, spending more time on the phone and MSN than getting to know her fellow students, then to realize this was ruining her student life (And who is this guy anyway?), and to break up with him around Christmas. This is a very common scenario, and although it puts a dampener on that first Christmas holiday, it usually means a much happier three years overall. Lennie is not one to follow predictable patterns though, and she has really broken the mould in this case – at the beginning of her third year she has herself a fiancé and has managed to enjoy her time at Birmingham to boot.

During my last visit to 'Brum', after Beth had left horribly early in the morning looking all professional in her nursing uniform, Lennie and I settled on her bed in our pyjamas with cups of tea and I got the whole scoop. So this is how the story went. She had a year off after school and before university, part of which she spent on a Christian discipleship course. Those on the course were forbidden to date anyone for the four months it lasted, which was not an issue to eighteen-year-old Lennie, who had managed to get through her teenage years without becoming boy-obsessed. Well, it wasn't an issue when she signed up anyway. Dan was a part of the church cell group she attended, and one evening he and his friend 'Magic Steve', so called for the magic tricks he could do, invited Lennie to join them for a trip to the cinema to see *Dawn of the Dead*. This was not even a spoof of a horror film, but a true horror film! She's a braver girl than I, who have been known to watch *Robin Hood, Prince of Thieves* through slitty eyes. (Okay – I admit they were closed tight shut, but only during the REALLY scary bits.) Lennie not only managed to tolerate this hard core cinematic experience, but even enjoyed it, earning her lots of points with the boys. And Dan had won favour in her eyes by the end of the evening, as he would have known if he'd understood that girls only throw popcorn at boys they like – at least that's what Lennie does.

Following the night of horror they saw each other a few times at the pub, where I imagine Magic Steve really came into his own, doing his tricks and entertaining everyone. On one of these occasions, Dan asked her about her thoughts on her future; what her plans and ambitions were and so on. Lennie happens to have a very well-formulated plan for what she wants to do with her life, and it involves counselling among other things. When he said he didn't know much about how counselling works, she demonstrated on him then and there, making him so flustered and uncomfortable that he blurted out his feelings for her. Given the rules of her course she was unsure what to do with this information and left the poor guy hanging with no hint of a response. She went away and thought about it, and spoke to her room-mate and her mentor but otherwise kept it quiet.

A few weekends later, the church was involved in a day of community service, culminating in a children's show for underprivileged kids on a housing estate. Part of the show was a game to win a soft toy duck. Lennie wanted the duck badly, and jumped up and down wildly until she was picked to go up on stage. The contestants had to select someone to join them up there, and she chose Dan. As they stuck pegs on each other's faces (for this was the price of the duck) she could see her course mentor glaring at her from the crowd. However, they did win, which was more important that any mentor's approval.

A 'define the relationship' conversation was becoming long overdue. When it eventually took place, they confessed their feelings for one another but decided to put everything on hold for the remaining three months of the course when Lennie would re-emerge into the world where people who like each other can date without fear of retribution. They made sure all relevant leaders knew about the situation and set about being patient and well behaved. It was all going fine until a guy on the same course kissed a sixteen-year-old girl in the church and on getting caught blamed his conduct on Lennie and Dan's situation. As a result they were called into a meeting like naughty kids and given even more stringent restrictions: 1. No time alone. 2. No talking about boyfriend/girlfriend things. 3. No seeing each other at all apart from at church or cell group. 4. No eye contact. 5. No feelings of affection. 6. No thoughts about anything romantic (I made up the last three!).

By the time the course was over, they were well and truly ready to become a couple. Their first official date happened at the first legal opportunity: the night the course ended. They went for a meal in a posh French restaurant and had a walk around a lake, and we can surmise that they happily broke rules one to six and quite rightly felt no guilt about the infringements whatsoever.

For the next year and a half they saw each other when they could, and although they both felt marrying each other was in their future, neither felt this was an option before Lennie graduated. They thought of themselves as 'engaged to be engaged' and just enjoyed the dating phase of their relationship as much as they could with the constant separations.

Although their relationship ran amazingly smoothly,

like all couples they had issues to work through and times when they wondered if they were supposed to be together. One of Lennie's niggles is that Dan spends one and a half hours in the bathroom each morning: yes, that's NINETY MINUTES! which amounts to ten and a half hours a week! And these marathons of cleanliness take place even on work days, when they require him to get up at 4.30 a.m. to fit them in! If they have a house with two bathrooms this might not be too much of a problem. One bathroom – and there would be some serious negotiating to be done I imagine.

As with any long-distance relationship, there was the occasional phone call that left them feeling cross and misunderstood and the odd less-than-blissful weekend which cast a disproportionately dark shadow because they weren't seeing each other every day. All their interactions were that much more intense because they were not able to live ordinary life together: their times together were precious and significant and either pulled the relationship forward several paces or held it back precariously.

Lennie describes herself as a worrier, and had lots of 'what if' questions. What if he stops loving me? What if we end up hating each other? What if we start arguing all the time? In the grand scheme of things, none of these niggles was anything like enough to cause the relationship to grind to a halt. She now says that although she had a bit of a block about the enormity of what marriage entails, it is actually the obvious thing to do for two people who love each other and have committed to continue to do so, and maybe not such a huge step to take after all.

Dan, according to Lennie, is terrible at secrets, so by the time it came to getting officially engaged she had managed to piece together his various hints and insinuations to form a pretty accurate picture of the when and where of the momentous event. They went to the Forest of Dean for the weekend, a place they had dreamed of living together one day, and on the Saturday morning Lennie got up really early, knowing this was to be the day, and sat in the bottom of their friends' garden with the dogs running around hunting rabbits, and she prayed and geared herself up for what was coming. They took a picnic and followed a sculpture trail through the forest. At lunchtime they found a fallen tree to sit on, and began eating their sandwiches. Dan suddenly said, 'Look, a horse!' and when she turned back to face him he was on one knee (the 'pesky horse' has turned up on several occasions throughout their time together, a source of major hilarity to them). Through a mouthful of sandwich she happily agreed to marry him.

The Pesky Horse and Other Good Reasons for Getting Engaged

Lennie and Dan are a real couple and not a prototype, so we won't dissect their relationship in a scientific manner to extract universal principles. Let me just explain, though, the reasons why I think they have been very sensible and commendable in the way they have gone about getting engaged.

When they first met there was a logistical problem – namely that Lennie was not allowed to date anyone under the terms of her programme. Whatever the rationale behind that rule, and however she might have felt about it, she respected the authority she was under and they waited to begin a relationship until it was above board. There are times for resisting and even fighting against circumstance, but there are also situations when waiting until the time is right is the honourable thing to do. Perhaps not many of you are signed up on courses that forbid you from dating, but you might well meet someone when they are involved with someone else, when they are not yet a Christian, when they need time and space to work on personal problems (that is not always a phoney brush-off!), when you are in a position of authority over them, such as being their teacher or youth leader, or any other circumstances which will resolve themselves, given time. In these cases, waiting is probably the right thing to be done, frustrating as it may seem. At worst, it will be a good character-developing exercise. At best, you will end up with a relationship you treasure because you have had to wait for it. In Genesis there is a story of a man named Jacob who worked for seven years to earn the hand in marriage of the woman he loved, Rachel, only to have her father con him into marrying her older sister Leah instead. Undeterred, he went on to work another seven years to ensure he could marry the one he had set his heart on. Jacob and Rachel must surely have enjoyed a passionate marriage after a wait like that.

There is no perfect length of time to date before getting engaged, but many people will tell you there is. On further questioning, this perfect time will probably turn out to be exactly the time they themselves dated before getting engaged, or the extreme opposite, depending on how happily married they are. Each couple will reach this point at their own pace – it might take a decade, it might take twenty minutes. The important factor is that they both reach the same point eventually and that they have taken the time they needed to get there. Lennie and Dan dated two years. This was exactly right for them.

Compatibility is a hard thing to quantify. That Lennie and Dan both find the 'pesky horse' very funny – is a sign that they are compatible with each other. It is really not as amusing to anyone else! It is not to do with being the same – it is something to do with being able to connect, to understand, to feel at home with that person, and to go about life with them in a way that feels natural and right.

I once went to a lecture on marriage in which the speaker said he tries to get the couples he sees for pre-marriage counselling to fight with each other. His point was that how conflict is handled is key in how successful a relationship is going to be: you need to have a few good fights and know you can resolve them before you are really ready to get engaged. I would definitely agree, but would want to add a reassurance that most of us (those of us who have friends who like us!) don't particularly relish fighting and learning to fight well is a lifelong challenge that we learn within marriage and certainly can't expect to master in a hurry.

Marriage Preparation

When you are deeply in love with someone and it isreci-procated and you are gazing ahead at a dreamy future with them, you can overlook certain hazards up ahead. Even though you may feel you have the healthiest, most enviable relationship in the history of 'True Love', some sort of marriage preparation is a sensible investment. It might even enhance your glorious smugness and make you feel yet more superior about your perfect twosome.

Shawn and I decided to do pre-engagement counselling, rather than marriage preparation. We figured
that it would be harder to pull out once the great cogs of
wedding planning began to turn, and we knew that
although it felt totally right for us to be together, there
were issues we could do with talking through in more
detail with an older, wiser moderator. We were set the
task of filling out a 'marriage expectation inventory' by
ourselves, sharing our answers with each other, then
going through them with our chosen guide, a wonderful
Regent professor who we both held in high esteem. The
inventory was mind bogglingly detailed. We went to a
coffee shop and spent several hours working on our
answers. I tried hard to peek at what Shawn was writing,
but without success. It covered ways of giving and receiving love, money and vocations, expectations of sex,
in-laws, spirituality, children, communication, time
management and leisure, and all of these in great depth.
Our professor said that sometimes he dreaded meeting
up with a couple after having read their questionnaires
but that he had been looking forward to seeing us, and
after carefully reading our answers, was happy to give us
his blessing to go ahead. Going through this process, of
course, didn't guarantee we would never face an unexpected difficulty, but it did give us confidence to know
that we had dug up as much trouble as we could find and
still wanted to get married.

If you want to do some sort of marriage preparation
there are plenty of ways to organize it. Many churches
offer the opportunity to meet up with a leader or a
mature married couple. Some lay on courses for engaged
couples, or you could buy a book on marriage and go
through it together. Whatever you decide to do, it is a

very good idea to have talked with each other in depth about the issues covered in the inventory I mentioned above – you don't want to be sprung with the surprising fact that your new wife wants six children half way through the honeymoon, when you have always thought one was a nice round number, or that your husband expects to make all the major decisions in your marriage because he is the man and you must submit, woman! A heads-up on these things would be helpful.

Questions

If your relationship has followed a tranquil and steady course, it is something to be heartily thankful for. Many people agonize over the decision to get married, or have to deal with opposition from families, or contend with less than ideal circumstances. A Canadian girl I knew married a Moroccan chap she met there on holiday. His first visa applications to Canada were turned down and they spent the initial four years of their marriage living thousands of miles apart. If your relationship seems pretty straightforward by comparison, maybe a part of you wonders if all this sensible predictability detracts a little from what will be your life's greatest romance – I wouldn't indulge that thought for long. It is a great blessing, and perhaps a bit miraculous, that you have found someone you want to spend the rest of your life with, and they want to spend the rest of their life with you too. What are the chances?

If you are in a steady and committed and happy relationship, chances are you will breeze through these questions. I hope they will be of some help even so:

1. Have you had some really good fights? How did you resolve them? (You did resolve them, right?)
2. Have timing and circumstance conspired to reassure you that you are doing the right thing? Have you had to overcome any obstacles to being together? What did you do with the rubble?
3. When have you had occasion to seek forgiveness from each other? How do you understand forgiveness, and what significance does it have in your relationship?
4. Have you thought about doing marriage preparation of some sort?
5. Who have you spoken to about your plans to get married? What was their response?

12

And They All Lived Happily Ever After

*Y*ou might have read this book because you are thinking about getting married, and maybe in the time it took you to get from the first page to the last, you came to a decision. If you decided to propose, or accept a proposal: Congratulations! Yippee! Hooray! Whatever the path that brought you to this point, you have arrived at an exciting stage in the journey, and adventure lies ahead.

Marriage is a wonderful invention. When it works well, it gives us intimacy, security, companionship and someone to share the household chores. I know without a doubt that my life is richer and better now that I share it with Shawn (as well as much more complicated and challenging!). But as you get swept up in the whirlpool of wedding planning, and the headiness of romantic schemes for your future together, remember that real life is going to continue, and real life is complicated. An engagement is not the end of the story, but a chapter somewhere near the beginning. Whether you believe you are the best suited couple since man first laid eyes on woman, or whether you are going for it with gritted teeth and knots in your stomach, you will find there are times you are happier than you thought you could ever be, and times when you wonder why on earth you married this infuriating and perplexing person eating dinner across the table from you with such appallingly bad table manners. Marriage takes work, perseverance, a willingness to forgive, and a determination to let yourself be known, however uncomfortable this exposure may be. May God bless you as you step up to the challenge.

One last word to the newly affianced among you: engagement is a funny stage in a relationship. You have decided you are ready to get married, and then you hang around waiting for it to happen, and it can be very frustrating and strange. Every time you have a conflict, and there is plenty to fight about, what with the wedding budget and the in-laws-in-waiting getting stuck in to the fray, you wonder if you should get out while you can. When you are all loved-up and happy together, it is torturous to say goodnight and go home to separate houses. If you haven't set the date yet, I strongly advise you to consider a week on Saturday – the weather is supposed to be sunny and warm and the vicar has a window in his schedule around 2 p.m. Perfect!

If you have decided that you aren't going to get engaged to your boyfriend or girlfriend, life may look quite bleak right now. A break-up is usually a sad and traumatic thing to go through, and you might take a while to recover. But however horrible it might feel right now, it is nothing compared to the misery of a difficult marriage or a divorce. So take heart – in the long run you will thank yourself.

Finding yourself single again suddenly can be scary. You might wonder if you will ever meet someone who is right for you. The fact is, if you want to get married one day, the likelihood is you will – most people do. But in the meantime, you need to work on discovering contentment in the present, in the circumstances you are in. Marriage, for all its benefits, is not the be all and end all of life. People have good days and bad days, married or single, and if you discover the truth of this now, you will not bring unrealistic expectations into your next relationship. I am sorry for your sadness and your broken heart, but I salute you for your courage.

These days we hear much about the decline of marriage. I have introduced you to twelve couples (eleven with their own chapters, and Shawn and I as extras) who made the decision to get married in the face of cultural pessimism, and who are, in a real-life kind of way, living happily ever after. I hope their stories have served to encourage, inspire and entertain.

The End